Jack Nicholson

Titles in the Series:

Jack Nicholson

Derek Sylvester

PROTEUS BOOKS

PROTEUS BOOKS is an imprint of
The Proteus Publishing Group

United States
PROTEUS PUBLISHING CO., INC.
733 Third Avenue
New York, N.Y. 10017
distributed by:
THE SCRIBNER BOOK COMPANIES, INC.
597 Fifth Avenue
New York, N.Y. 10017

United Kingdom
PROTEUS (PUBLISHING) LIMITED
Bremar House,
Sale Place,
London, W2 1PT.

ISBN 0 86276 014 3 p/b
       0 86276 029 1 h/b

First published 1982

Editor MICHAEL BRECHER
Typeset AGP (TYPESETTING) LTD.
Printed & Bound in Italy by
NEW INTERLITHO S.P.A., Milan.

Contents

PREFACE

Of the seven decades of Hollywood history, it's oddly the Fifties that strike us today as dated beyond recall. To be sure, the great majority of spectators — whose interest in cinema, restricted to new movies as they surface week by week, is an unthinkingly topical one — would be puzzled by the notion that the medium might have a past worth investigating. Faced with a black and white movie they have the impression of being color blind, with a silent of being struck deaf. Obsolete acting styles can still provoke incredulous giggles, even in the context of an art-house revival. Ditto for primitive (though, from an esthetic viewpoint, not necessarily inferior) technical processes. Television companies are bombarded with complaints after the screening of any work, however widely recognized as a classic, made before World War II. Yet, even if for the genuine buff old movies can possess an endearing patina that is frustratingly absent from more recent efforts, the Fifties contrive to seem both too close and too distant: too close to be filtered through the rosy spectacles of nostalgia, too distant to compete with the latest big-budget productions. Costumes appear ill-fitting, colors garish, psychological attitudes preposterously outmoded. In particular, the actors all appear to be much too old.

Though one can name a cluster of significant movies about and presumably for the younger generation — Laslo Benedek's *The Wild One*, starring a leather-jacketed, monumentally brooding Marlon Brando, Nicholas Ray's *Rebel Without A Cause* with James Dean, and Richard Brooks' *Blackboard Jungle* at once spring to mind — most of them were made not only by adults (this was before the Movie Brat era, when the well-dressed director was wearing jodhpurs, not diapers) but with the express purpose of confirming *adult* prejudices about youth. Typical protagonists (often played by actors of indeterminate age) were wide-eyed teenagers, crew-cut, clean-cut and almost comic-cut, whose overriding ambition was to be selected for the college football team; or else, if from the other side of the track, ghetto hoodlums teased out of their delinquency by the homespun therapy of some nice, understanding, hypersensitive grown-up (such as Glenn Ford's high school teacher in Brooks' film).

Even in offerings without any youth theme, many of the characters looked suspiciously more advanced in years than seemed called for by the plot. Hollywood's greatest stars had grown old with the movies themselves and — not surprisingly — a statutory retirement age had never been on the cards. By the middle of the decade James Stewart was 52, John Wayne 53. Henry Fonda was 55, Cary Grant a year older (and though he could pass for considerably younger, much of his Peter Pan charm depended on the contrast between that youthfulness and our knowledge that he was well into maturity).

Still half-consciously, young people were beginning to feel that they had been excluded from the movies, that their generation (which had not yet acquired a unique, representative 'voice') should be given more prime time on the screen. And what gave this feeling clout was the fact that, at least in potential, they were becoming a public to reckon with. Statistically, as the generation of the immediate postwar baby boom, they comprised a larger percentage of the national population than ever before; and since the bland Eisenhower years (perceived as 'the good old days' even as they were being lived) also witnessed an unprecedented financial boom, they suddenly had money in their pockets. Money which they, unlike their TV-worshipping parents, were prepared to spend in the cinema: movie attendances were inexorably sliding down the age scale. When the missing 'voice' was finally heard, mobilizing millions of teenagers across the nation, it turned out to be that of a pudgy but smouldering rock 'n' roll singer from Memphis, Elvis Presley. Youth had discovered its own music — now it wanted its own movies and movie stars.

For the first time since the advent of the talkies in 1929, a whole new breed of actors and actresses rose to prominence in Hollywood. So radical was the turnover that by the mid-Seventies the American cinema was populated almost exclusively by performers who had been unknown less than ten years before; the few older actors still in harness were kicked upstairs, as if were, to so-called 'guest' stardom in disaster movies. (Never board a plane if Olivia De Havilland or Joseph Cotton, Ava Gardner or Burt Lancaster are listed among the passengers!)

Who are these new stars? Why are they new and why are they stars? From the blond ruggedness of Robert Redford to the sassy Broadway chutzpah of Barbra Streisland, from the tough guy vulnerability of Dustin Hoffman to the radical chi-chi of Jane Fonda, from the tormented macho intensity of Robert De Niro to the fragile elfin glitter of Liza Minnelli, they have proved no less versatile than Hollywood's older guard. Just as a change of audience brought about a change of actors, so these actors have changed the nature of the movies in which they have become involved. Though such emblematic Seventies works as Martin Scorsese's *Taxi Driver*, Bob Fosse's *Cabaret* and Francis Coppola's *Apocalypse Now* can be aligned with traditional, not to say well-worn, genres (respectively, the urban thriller, musical and war movie), their extreme violence and sexual candor would have been unthinkable in earlier decades. Even James Cagney, in some murky Warners melodrama, was never called upon to defend an underage junkie prostitute as De Niro does in *Taxi Driver*. Nor did Betty Grable ever give her all in a nightclub as seedy as that of *Cabaret*. As for John Wayne as the Kurtz of *Apocalypse Now*...! Remarkable, too, is that, while Hollywood's biggest box-office triumphs — George Lucas' *Star Wars*, Steven Spielberg's *Jaws* and *Close Encounters of the Third Kind* and Richard Donner's *Superman* — depend less on star names than on a barrage of highly sophisticated technology, this new breed of actors has opted to appear in movies with recognizably serious themes, thereby allowing them to remain a viable proposition. As Gloria Swanson's crazed silent movie star diva could claim in *Sunset Boulevard*, 'We didn't need voices! We had *faces*!', so they will be able to say, 'We didn't need special effects — we had *talent*!'

If any one man laid the groundwork for that talent, it was of course Brando, whose influence on such actors as Hoffman, Pacino, De Niro, Hackman and Richard Gere has been immeasurable. Riding into a Hollywood sunset on the motorcycle of *The Wild One* back in 1953, he totally transformed the surrounding landscape. It is because of this, because an exception can hardly be an example, that he has remained a special case, perhaps the greatest of all American film actors. It was fifteen years later that another, more easily identifiable precursor of the new breed appeared, also on a motorcycle, as a soft-spoken, alcoholically befuddled Southern lawyer in Dennis Hopper's *Easy Rider*. He was Jack Nicholson.

Nicholson is a true precursor, not only because, like the character he played, he'd been around and it showed on his sharp, humorous, world-weary features, but also because, unlike the unique Brando (the two syllables of whose name resound as eerily as those of Garbo), unlike the rising young stars who followed him, he bestrode two distinct generations of acting styles. He possessed the pugnacity of a Cagney, the virility of a Garfield, the diabolic charm of a Gable. He could be as suavely droll as Cary Grant, as gee-shucks and gangling as James Stewart, as moody and introspective as Paul Muni. He could appear both magnetically attractive and malevolently ugly (on occasion within the space of a single film, such as Stanley Kubrick's *The Shining*). At the same time, he was without any doubt an embodiment of the Seventies and remains so of the Eighties. In other words, the most *indispensable* actor of modern American cinema.

What makes him so sympathetic, in an age of facile overnight success, is that stardom came slowly to him. Before his revelatory appearance in *Easy Rider* (whose true stars, it should be recalled, were Peter Fonda and Hopper himself), he had played mostly small, unremarkable and unremarked roles in no fewer than *nineteen* movies. In a way, his career had begun more like a director's, like that of one of the Movie Brats, De Palma, Coppola, Spielberg and Lucas — who served their apprenticeships with routine assignments on exploitation movies and the odd scriptwriting chore for Roger Corman. It was this experience, however uninspiring at the time, that later enabled him to turn to the direction of *Drive, He Said* (1970) and *Goin' South* (1978), with a wholly professional assurance. Ask any film buff to list Nicholson's appearances on film and he will probably include *Drive, He Said*, which he directed only: for so indelibly has his personality been stamped on its imagery that one almost recalls certain lines of dialogue spoken in his voice.

Another factor which would seem to distinguish him from his fellow actors (as witness numerous interviews) is his intelligence. Nicholson is blessed with the capacity, rare in anyone and uncannily so in an actor, to size himself up with neither undue modesty nor that brand of coy frankness which journalists term 'disarming'. Before subjecting his life and work to biographical study, it might be worth quoting him for a demonstration of how succinctly he has been able to define not only himself but his 'image', both sides of the mirror (or screen) at once:

'I think people believe that I'm fairly uncompromising, that I have a certain vitality about what I do, that I'm almost, at such an early age, iconoclastic in my attachment for individuality, where the only movement in that sector is away from it, really. I think that they know that I'm

capable of making a large horse's ass out of myself because, for people who like me, I translate into a kind of honest vulnerability which comes not from constantly attempting to solidify my position. I don't hit something, then drive it in more times to make sure it's there. I hope and believe that people sense that I'm honestly interested, though possibly more cynical than they'd like, about all of our lives — if you can stand that sort of pretentious capsulization. And they're right. I think they're right about all of that.

'I think they have a slightly more flamboyant picture of me than I actually am — I don't object to that at all. I've always hated to think it was true, but it probably is true that people older than me have a slightly more negative picture of me than do younger people, because to older people I'm fairly radical, to younger people I'm fairly comfortable. Someone 50 thinks I'm a dope fiend, someone 15 thinks I'm a mild kind of guy.'

"NO NOVOCAINE! IT DULLS THE SENSES."

On April 22 1937, New York's Radio City Music Hall premièred a new movie, William Wellman's *A Star is Born* with Fredric March and Janet Gaynor. Just a few miles south on the New Jersey coastline, in a small Neptune City hospital, a star *was* born. Though a star's death is calculated to make headlines nationwide, his entry into the world will generally go unrecorded; and the circumstances of Jack Nicholson's birth were even less propitious than those of the aspiring unknown played by Miss Gaynor in Wellman's film. He was raised as the only son of Ethel May and John Nicholson whose two daughters, June and Lorraine, were aged 17 and 14 respectively at his birth.

John Nicholson, whose antecedents hailed from County Cork, was a sign painter and part-time window dresser — and, by Jack's own account, very much a part-time husband. Separated from his wife in all but name, he soon moved out of their lower middle-class home, drifted aimlessly but never entirely vanished from the scene, like some forlorn figure in an American Gothic painting for whom the artist cannot quite decide which would be the best position. He was an incorrigible alcoholic, incapable of walking in a straight line past a bar or along the floor of a precinct station. Jack would sometimes accompany him on his bar crawls, drinking endless sarsparillas while he consumed twice as many raw brandies. Oddly, Jack never expressed any bitterness at his father's failure as a provider. He once described him as 'a quiet, melancholy, tragic figure — a very soft man', and undoubtedly exploited memories of him for his own subsequent portrayals of failed drifters still clinging to the remnants of their own battered dignity. As he himself put it: 'The search for me and for the character is compulsive. There's never been a time in my life when that wasn't going on. I suppose it's partly the coincidence of when I was born and where, plus whatever fantasies I have as a person.'

It was up to Ethel May to raise the family on her own, a task that might have daunted many women during the Depression but which she undertook with unflagging energy and good humor. Trained as a beautician, but unable to afford the luxury of a real beauty salon, she hit upon the simple expedient of operating one from home. Even when the business thrived, instead of opening a salon downtown, the family chose to move into a more spacious house.

Though a reasonably normal child, Jack early acquired one habit that tenaciously persists to this day: that of never addressing friends or relatives by their names if a suitable nickname could be found. And before you could say . . . well, 'Jack Nicholson', he would find one. Thus, Ethel May's name was soon 'Mud', Lorraine's

"Teenage Rebel to Mad-Dog Killer" J.N., Jordan Whitefield and Barbara Knudson in *Cry Baby Killer*

". . . a cliché-ridden cautionary tale . . ." J.N. in trouble in *Too Soon to Love*

easily contracted to 'Rain' and her husband George, somewhat to his chagrin, was forever known as 'Shorty'. (If June alone was spared such humiliation, it was because, when Jack was only four, she left home to become a showgirl with the Earl Carroll Vanities in Miami.) More recently, his long-term companion Anjelica Huston (the daughter of director John) has become for some unfathomable reason 'Toolman', Candice Bergen responds (or doesn't, as the case may be) to 'Bug', Mike Nichols, who directed Jack in *Carnal Knowledge* and *The Fortune*, to 'Big Nick', Peter Fonda to 'The Bike', Art Garfunkel to 'Art the Garf' and Warren Beatty, rather disappointingly, to 'Master B'.

He also distinguished himself as a child by an exceptional capacity for being mean and stubborn if thwarted in some cherished project. His tantrums were notorious. Whenever he was punished, he would stomp upstairs, creating such an unholy commotion as to make the ladies under the driers drop their *Saturday Evening Posts* in fright. He would tear the sheets off his bed, rip up the curtains, slam one door after another, then either scream out 'for cripes sake!' or lapse into a convulsive mutism. But though Mud's hand would sometimes deal him a painful slap, Jack's grin was what is called an 'infectious' one and no one could for long stay angry with him. That grin, which became his ambiguous trademark, makes one think of Chaucer's arresting phrase 'the smiler with a knife' — except that in Nicholson's case the smile and the knife are one. It's a weapon which he has learned to wield with the dexterity of a Jim Bowie.

Jack's first school was Roosevelt Elementary in Neptune City. There he proved to be a straight A student, a leading light of the baseball team and already something of a diminutive con man. His teachers recall how, if any of his most prized possessions had been confiscated after some minor misdemeanor, he would proceed to charm the living daylights out of its confiscator. It was almost as if he sought out trouble in order to demonstrate just how swiftly he could extricate himself from it. Acting up is also a form of acting.

On one occasion, relegated to the dunce's corner of the classroom for what he later called 'a problem in deportment', he gave himself the lugubrious appearance of an Auguste, or white clown, by powdering his face with chalk dust. Such buffoonery was a defense mechanism against his chronic self-consciousness, especially in mixed company. Jack, a short, chubby kid, was careful at school dances to calculate every possible risk of a rebuff before finally settling on a partner. More universally liked than inspiring any individual 'crush', he was at ease in group

activities, of which he was invariably the instigator. The graduation party, for example. The little girls resplendent in their formal party dresses, the little boys no less so in their Sunday best. And when roses were casually suggested as a decoration for the party venue, it was Jack who organized a group of friends to 'deflower' the neighbourhood gardens during the night. He even arranged for a surprise cake to be baked for one little girl whose birthday it happened to be. If an actor can be described as someone who is paid to 'show off', then the twelve-year old Jack was already an amateur actor.

At Manasquan High School, Jack was again a candidate for election as Most Popular Boy in his class; and, as the manager of the varsity basketball team in his freshman year, also the one Most Likely to Succeed. Though he was suspended three times — for swearing, for smoking on school grounds and once for destroying scoreboard equipment belonging to a visiting team suspected of cheating — the offences were minor, the punishments gracefully accepted and soon forgiven. The fact, too, that he had excellent grades ('top 2% nationally,' he later claimed) may have contributed to his popularity with the teaching personnel. But already, bored with schooling and toying only half-heartedly with the notion of accepting a chemical engineering scholarship to the University of Delaware, Jack had what might be termed a two-track mind. Sex and showbusiness. His experience of the former much advanced by the speed with which he grew out of his unsightly puppy fatness, he began to date girls as regularly then as he has done since. To journalists from *Screw* magazine he could describe with disturbingly total recall his very first wet dream, which involved a naked young woman in a forest slowly unzipping his flies — and this while he was still in short pants!

As for showbiz, his unofficial début had taken place on the stage of Roosevelt Grammar School, where he belted out 'Managua Nicaragua' in front of parents and staff. Already a keen movie fan, he predictably numbered Brando, Clift and Dean among his idols. Before finally making up his mind about college, he decided to spend the summer with his 'sister' June, who had divorced her husband and settled in North Hollywood with their two children.

Hollywood, 1954: a community whose streets were paved not with gold but with stars. Easy enough to imagine the naive young visitor from New Jersey, in his D.A. quiff and tight, tight jeans, strolling along Hollywood Boulevard, stopping mesmerised at each paving-stone engraved with the name of one of Hollywood's

"Antonioni doesn't make dramatic constructions, he makes configurations" J.N. and Maria Schneider in *The Passenger*

luminaries. Or examining the cement footprints outside Grauman's Chinese Theater, footprints in whose footsteps he hoped to follow. But in the mid-fifties Hollywood was in the throes of its own Depression. To paraphrase a celebrated piece of doggerel verse:

> Big screens have little screens
> Upon their backs to bite 'em;
> Little screens have smaller screens,
> And so ad infinitum.

Television was making such inroads into Hollywood's hegemony that all those beautiful blondes studiously sipping malted milks at Schwabs Drugstore in the hope of being discovered by a talent scout often ended up serving behind the counter.

Jack had come, he had seen, and he had been conquered. This, he knew, was where he wanted to be. Inside the magical magnet. All talk of Delaware University and of becoming a chemical engineer faded away. But a boy soprano rendering of 'Managua Nicaragua', however much it might have wowed 'em back in Neptune City, was scarcely calculated to have Hollywood's studio gates swinging open in deference. So, like thousands of hopefuls before him, he took a series of dead-end jobs allowing him simply to bide his time. He was a salesman in a toy store, a hustler in a poolhall. 'I could make money being the third best player in the room. I made some money at the track, too. I bought my first car with it, a '49 Studebaker.' Like so many others, too, after five or six months he was forced into a heartbreaking decision to return home, even getting as far as purchasing a plane ticket. But it was then, at the very last moment, that there came a turning point in his life, the kind every aspiring move actor dreams of but which only ever seems to happen in the movies themselves. He managed, almost without trying, to obtain a job as mailboy in Metro-Goldwyn-Mayer's cartoon department, handling Tom and Jerry's fan letters for 30 dollars a week.

Not much, perhaps, but it was a start. Enough to allow Jack to 'go Hollywood'. He read *The Catcher in the Rye*, the then fashionable Existentialists and classic Zen Buddhist texts. He discovered an affinity with black cultures (indirectly dating from his basketball days) and the burgeoning Beat movement. And, never one to waste time, he immediately set about turning himself into an actor. 'They told me my neck was too long. At one interview I had, the man said, "Gee, Jack, I don't really know what we could use you for, but when we do need you, we'll really need you."' Absolutely devoid of experience,

"...a generation of born losers..." J.N. in *Studs Lonigan*

he relied as usual on his smile, attracting the attention of at least one genial studio executive, Joe Pasternak, the producer of *Anchors Aweigh*, *The Great Caruso*, *Love Me or Leave Me* among many other examples of well-upholstered corn. Pasternak arranged for a screen test which Jack, who had failed to memorize his dialogue, flunked miserably. When he and Pasternak met afterwards in the mailroom, however, the latter conveniently appeared to have forgotten the incident and was prepared to encourage Jack all over again. This time around, he secured his protégé a place in a local workshop theater called the Player's Ring.

Though he was offered a few minor roles — in *Tea and Sympathy*, for example — what Jack remembered most gratefully about this phase of his career was the opportunity it gave him to mix with other young actors, writers and directors. He concientiously enrolled in a beginner's acting course run by Jeff Corey, whose students included James Coburn, Sally Kellerman (later 'Hot Lips' in Robert Altman's movie *M.A.S.H*), producer-director Roger Corman and writer Robert Towne (who would be responsible for the screenplays of two of Jack's most successful films, *The Last Detail* and *Chinatown*, and with whom he shared a tiny apartment in the outer reaches of Hollywood). But awe never came easily to Jack Nicholson. Once, when Corey admonished him to 'show me some poetry', an already confident tyro snapped back, 'Maybe, Jeff, you don't see the poetry I'm showing you.' Another close, and long-lasting, friendship was struck with Robert Vaughn, whose Method classes couldn't have been very suitable for his best-known role as *The Man From U.N.C.L.E.*.

This whole period was crucial to Jack's development. To a *Playboy* interviewer, he summed it up as 'a time of freshness and a discovery of what acting was all about, of meeting new people and being inspired by other people's work, of watching an actor or an actress who could hardly talk come into a class and then six months later suddenly do a brilliant scene.' 'Six months later ... suddenly ...' The contradiction, certainly applicable to Jack's own career, is only an apparent one in Hollywood, where 'luck' might be something you work on for years, and 'overnight' success the culmination of decade's failures.

When he joined the Player's Ring, this tiny repertory theater boasted nothing in the way of production values. Even floorboards had to be removed at night from some local timber yard. Toilets were purloined from gas stations, lighting equipment from all-night supermarkets. Yet so high-spirited was the company's youthful mayhem that it must even then have seemed appealing — except, maybe, if you were hoping to go to the toilet in a gas station. There were parties, too, with surreptitious drug-taking and communal jaunts to such long forgotten L.A. watering holes as the Unicorn, the Renaissance and Chez Paulette. Though he seldom touched hard liquor, Jack would lay in gallons of inexpensive Californian wine: again to *Playboy*, 'Harry Dean Stanton, who was one of my close sidekicks in those days' (and whose name is used fetishistically in almost every one of his movies) 'says that whenever he thinks of me in that period, he always sees me with a cheap red wine on my red lips.' An aptly Wildean description for someone who would go to a party looking as angelic as Dorian Gray and wake up next morning (or afternoon) bearing a striking resemblance to his portrait.

Meanwhile, MGM had closed down its cartoon department, making Jack redundant along with Tom and Jerry. Even if his most frequent, and longest running, engagement during these lean years was at the unemployment office, he was beginning to land minor roles on television, on such shows as *Divorce Court* and *Matinee Theater*. Then in 1957 a young independent producer-director, Roger Corman, in the process of casting his next movie, remembered Jack from Jeff Corey's acting classes and signed him up for the lead in *Cry Baby Killer* (1958)

It might be instructive for a moment to consider the unique career of Corman, who singlehandedly transformed the margin into the mainstream of contemporary American cinema. Termed 'the Orson Welles of Z pictures' by the *Sight and Sound* critic Peter John Dyer, he had already churned out such ephemera as *The Day the World Ended*, *Swamp Women*, *It Conquered the World*, *Not of this Earth*, *The Undead*, *The She-Gods of Shark Reef* and *Attack of the Crab Monsters*. If nothing in these movies quite lived up to the outrageous promise of their titles, it was because the titles were usually Corman's primary inspiration; afterwards, poorly paid but enthusiastic young writers were set to work turning them into commercial projects. The extraordinary vitality of Corman's output derives precisely from his cavalier disregard of high art, or even major studio, priorities. Since much less money was at stake, greater risks could be taken with the material; and since the movies were often shot and edited in under a month, their narratives were characterized by a New Wave looseness that offered a refreshing antidote to the expensive academicism that too frequently dogged more prestigious productions of the same period. Junk food it may have been, but it was preferable to the pretty but

J.N. in Tony Richardson's *The Border*

tasteless haute cuisine served up by the studios. Interestingly, many of the young moviemakers who slaved in Corman's kitchens have since become Hollywood's most desirable properties: Coppola, Spielberg and Lucas (albeit, less interestingly, continuing sometimes to make what can only be described as blockbusting B movies, such as the Lucas/Spielberg collaboration *Raiders of the Lost Ark*).

Cry Baby Killer, directed by one Jus Addis, was a typical Corman product (but then, Corman's films were never other than 'typical'). Shot in just ten days for a total cost of 7,000 dollars, a sum that wouldn't have paid for a single ad for *Raiders of the Lost Ark*, its own slogan screamed out rather misleadingly 'Teenage Rebel to Mad-Dog Killer!'. The perfunctory plotline centered on Jimmy, a high school kid aggressed at a drive-in by two hoodlums who have been ogling his girlfriend. Thinking he has killed them in the ensuing scuffle, Jimmy holes up in a storeroom with a terrified mother and child as his hostages. The police move in, TV cameras focus on the siege, and the growing crowd of onlookers is soon catered to by vendors of hot dogs and soft drinks. All ends predictably, however, with the last-minute rescue of the hostages and Jimmy's discovery that his plea of self-defense has been accepted.

Apart from some vapid, clumsily handled attempts at satire, directed against just those excesses of mob voyeurism to which the movie pandered, *Cry Baby Killer* was basically a crude exercise in suspense; the theme of a siege was chosen mainly because it would limit the action — and thus, expenses — to a single set. Nicholson, however, made an extremely persuasive debut (though hindsight, and the future course of his career, may be coloring one's view). Since the scenarist's primary concern was to lead the plot from A to Z without concerning himself too much with the letters in between, he was provided with little on which to build a real performance or develop character. But he brooded very photogenically, and, if his admiration for Brando and Dean was sometimes allowed to topple over into imitation, there was a steely charm about his presence that boded well.

Jack himself evidently thought so. For one brief, fanciful moment he was convinced that superstardom was within his grasp. Yet it wasn't until 1960 that Corman cast him in another film, *The Little Shop of Horrors*. This is what is loosely what is termed a 'cult movie': i.e. though liked by few people, those few people like it a lot. Oddly enough, Jack received no billing; oddly, because he was given a memorable, if peripheral, role as a masochistic dental patient who gurgles

'No novocaine! It dulls the senses' and squeals in pleasurable anticipation when the dentist gloats, 'This is going to hurt you more than it does me!' For the rest, it was an amiable, knowing horror movie spoof about a timid florist (Jonathon Haze) and his feverish quest for human flesh as fodder for the voraciously carniverous plant which he is raising in his employer's flower shop. The plant itself turned out to be endearingly tatty, troubled by digestive problems — it would swallow a gunman whole with much appreciative smacking of its petal-like lips but regurgitate his gun with an embarrassed belch — and as insatiable as a newborn babe. The movie shamelessly flaunted its Poverty Row sets; and if any amusing idea, however irrelevant, occured to the scenarist Charles B. Griffiths, he would insert it in the script without a moment's hesitation.

During 1960, Jack made three other screen appearances in rapid succession, very much in a similar mould. 'I always played psychos or the boy next door. There were a lot of juvenile-delinquent pictures in those days. I was usually some crumby, cruddy person.' On each occasion, he would fleetingly believe his chance had come, before finding himself back on square one. Which might explain the fact that, with Monte Hellman, who would later direct him in a matching pair of heavily symbolic Westerns, *The Shooting* and *Ride in the Whirlwind* (both 1966) he collaborated on an unfilmed screenplay based on the myth of Sisyphus.

In *Too Soon to Love*, a melodramatic quickie directed by Richard Rush (now celebrated for his 'metaphysical' Hollywood-on-Hollywood comedy, *The Stunt Man*, with Peter O'Toole), he played a buddy of the hero named . . . Buddy. The plot revolved around a couple of insipid teenage sweethearts, the girl's unwanted pregnancy, and the pair's involvement in petty crime to pay for an abortion. Though it can still be seen on the late late show, this cliché-ridden cautionary tale is strictly for incurable insomniacs. Of greater ambition was Irving Lerner's *Studs Lonigan*, an adaptation of the autobiographical trilogy of novels by the American realist writer James T. Farrell. The three books, written in the early Thirties, dealt with the gradual disillusionment of their wilful, aimless hero from the optimism of the Twenties into the Depression that followed. In the mosaic of incidents detailing the shift from youthful hope and self-confidence to gradual disenchantment, defeat and death, Studs himself personified the spiritual emptiness of a generation of born losers, haunting the sordid rain-swept sidewalks, bars and poolrooms of Chicago. To telescope such a sprawling nar-

Producer-director-whizzkid Roger Corman

rative into a film version lasting 100 minutes was a tall order, too tall as it happened for Lerner, a sociologist, anthropologist, former editor of documentaries and, at 51, an aging 'young' hope of the American cinema.

The movie was suffocated by a plangent, pervasive musical score reminiscent of Kurt Weill; though much of the social context which had enriched the novels' texture had been excised, the accompanying squalor — a wild party, a brutal sexual assault — was complacently lingered over by Haskell Wexler's camera; and, as the doomed protagonist, winsome all-American Christoper Knight invested the character with inappropriate soap opera 'sensitivity'. Moreover, instead of ending with Studs' tragic, futile death, as do the novels, Lerner opted to wheel in a loveable old priest (Jay C. Flippen),whose piously heartwarming sermon instantly converts our anti-hero to the finer things of life and shames him into returning to the girl he had made pregnant. In all, a sadly wasted opportunity, to which the novelist himself, in a forthright letter to the *New York Times*, took justified exception. As Weary Reilly, a member of the gang with which Studs hangs out, Nicholson was at least more effective than the luckless leading man; but in the crossfire of reviews, good and bad, which greeted the film,

his brief cameo went unremarked. He later claimed that he had landed the role because he was the only young actor in Hollywood with the stamina to wade through the trilogy's seven hundred densely packed pages.

His last 1960 movie, *The Wild Ride*, was again directed by Corman and featured Jack as Johnny Varron, a hot-rod gang leader whose recklessness causes several bloody deaths before the police catch up with him. Basically a reprise of his *Cry Baby Killer* persona, it furthered his career as little as it did the art of the cinema.

Of much greater import was a watershed in his private life. At one of Corey's classes, which he was still assiduously attending, Jack met Sandra Knight, a pretty dark-haired actress who had worked mostly in television. After a number of regular dates, they married and moved into a charming house whose furniture, while not strictly antique, could be described as comfortably 'old'. In the following year, 1963, their daughter Jennifer was born. 'We were very much in love,' said Jack, 'and I took the vows totally at ease.' For the moment, at least, the hectic hedonism which had marked his lifestyle since he had arrived in Hollywood was at an end. Another episode, of a diametrically opposed nature, also contributed to sobering him up and forcing him to take a long hard look at his future.

June, in whom he had never ceased to confide, was stricken with cancer. When, in the company of 'Mud' and 'Rain', Jack visited her in the Cedars of Lebanon Hospital just before she died, he was horrified by the decline in her physical condition: June had lost over 40 pounds in a few months and was suffering incessant pain. Though they had remained close over the years, her death affected him more than he thought possible (and perhaps more than was normal for a brother): he broke down and sobbed uncontrollably in the corridor of the hospital.

In 1962 Jack was offered a part in *The Broken Land*, directed by John Bushelman. A 'psychological' Western, as was then the rage, its CinemaScope format (unusual for a routine 60-minute programmer) only gave the director greater latitude to display his debilitating lack of visual style. Jack was cast as Will Broicous, the offspring of a notorious outlaw, at odds with a sadistic Marshal (Kent Smith) who evidently believed that the sins of the father should be atoned for by the punishment of the son. Like the scenarist before him, Jack was unable to make much of the role; and like the audience after him, the best he could do was write off the whole fiasco as experience. In 1963, however, he returned to the Corman fold to play a character called Rexford Bedlo — what weird names the

poor man was saddled with — in an 'adaptation' of Edgar Allen Poe's narrative poem, *The Raven*. Corman filmed no fewer than eight of Poe's *Tales of Mystery and Imagination* — most notably, *The Fall of the House of Usher*, *The Mask of the Red Death* and *The Tomb of Ligeia*, all starring a suavely demented Vincent Price — and though the imagination involved was usually Corman's own and the mystery sometimes why Poe's name was attached to them at all, these movies remain among the liveliest and most entertaining examples of campy Gothick romance ever made in Hollywood.

The Raven was more overtly parodic than in others of the cycle: assembling Boris Karloff, Peter Lorre and the ubiquitous Price as three bloodthirsty sorcerers, it bore as much resemblance to the literary original as its star trio did to the Andrews Sisters. The eponymous bird flutters in at the window and Price, seeking oracular knowledge as to the precise location of his deceased wife in the hereafter, is greeted with a snappish 'How the hell should I know!': as he explains that the coffin containing her corpse has been given pride of place in the living room, Lorre mutters impatiently, 'Where else?'; and one of the more delicate ingredients for a secret potion turns out to be 'entrails of troubled horse'. As Price's son and the movie's juvenile lead,

J.N. as a "hot-rod gang leader" in *The Wild Ride*

J.N. on the road in *The Postman Always Rings Twice*

Nicholson was clearly ill-at-ease with such Grand Guignol high jinks. Beside the three leads, who could have played their parts in their sleep, he looked as if that was exactly what he was doing. The rich color photography, as usual with Corman, was by Floyd Crosby and the consistently amusing screenplay by the science-fiction novelist, Richard Matheson.

In October of the same year, Nicholson and Karloff were reunited in an extraordinary film, *The Terror*. Extraordinary less for its very variable quality than because of a shooting schedule that was economical even by Corman's standards. It was shot in just three days, plus a weekend for the (surprisingly attractive) exteriors, with hand-me-down costumes and décors which Corman had already rented and didn't like to see go unused. Such rapidity left no time for dialogue and acting rehearsals, an omission painfully obvious from the end result. Not based on Poe though exploiting the same ghoulish atmosphere (complete with liberal swathes of dry ice curling around the actors' feet), its confused plot recounted the pursuit of an elusive, ethereal maiden by a Napoleonic cavalry officer, André Duvalier (Nicholson, a victim of miscasting yet again). His search leads him to the fog-shrouded castle of the Baron von Leppe (a rather weary Karloff), in whose deepest, cobwebbiest crypt he finally embraces his zombie-like inamorata, only to have her decompose all over his epaulettes. Since, as written, Duvalier was intended less to be played than to be hammed up as outrageously as possible, Nicholson proved quite as stilted and wooden as in *The Raven*, his discomfort doubtless aggravated by the fact that his wife Sandra had been cast as the mysterious, otherworldly heroine. (She quit the movies soon after.)

Karloff had been scaring audiences out of their wits for over three decades, and the years were beginning to take their toll. In *The Terror* his dignified weather-beaten features were not so much those of a raging necrophiliac as of the kindly old English gentleman with a passion for cricket that he was in private life. (Significantly, it was this ambiguity in his performance that attracted Peter Bogdanovich when he made his début as a director in 1967 with *Targets*. He cast Karloff as Byron Orlock, a veteran horror movie star who realises that the mad magician nightmares which are his stock in trade can no longer compete with a more contemporary brand of horror, the kind that stalks suburban estates and shopping malls. In the film's drive-in climax where the two horrors, Orlock and a mentally deranged young sniper, confront head on, what is being screened is precisely *The Terror*.)

Though the movie's credits listed mainly unknowns, they can be seen to have been retroactively somewhat starry. The director's assistant was Monte Hellman and the baffling rank of associate producer was held by none other than Francis Coppola, the future wonder boy of *The Godfathers I and II* and *Apocalypse Now*. During that frantic week of shooting, even Jack was permitted to direct a few scenes. *The Terror*, however lowly its place in film history, was for him a crossroads between past and future, anonymity and stardom. Jack never forgot what he owed to Corman: 'Look at the directors who've worked through Roger's system: Francis Coppola, Monte Hellman, Irving Kershner, myself, Dennis Hopper, Bogdanovich, etc. What directors have the major studios produced? You can see right away that the guy's a superior person. He's the best producer I've met in the business. The man carried me for seven

"...campy Gothick romance..." J.N. with Peter Lorre, Vincent Price and Hazel Court in *The Raven*

J.N. with Dianna Darrin in "a 'psychological' Western" *Broken Land*

J.N., "stilted and wooden" in *The Terror* with his then wife Sandra Knight

years. I feel tremendously indebted to him, but there's no emotional blackmail involved. *He* doesn't feel that I'm indebted to him. He's the only man in the movie business for whom, if he said, "You got a deal," I'd write a check without seeing the movie. He's that honest.'

"THE BULLETS DON'T KILL YA, YA DIE OF BLOOD POISONING!"

Jack's career was ticking over steadily (even if you had to strain to hear it), but he himself was bored. He dreaded to think of himself becoming established as a 'supporting performer', condemned to endless reprisals of André Duvalier; if juvenile delinquents — his forte, after all — are often psychologically ill-prepared for the advent of middle age, no less are actors who specialize in playing them on screen. As a husband, father and breadwinner, however, he couldn't afford to turn any part down, no matter how unsuited it might be to his particular gifts. Being choosy is a star's privilege, one which he wouldn't hesitate to take advantage of when he finally achieved stardom: his career has been the most intelligently handled in contemporary Hollywood. But, as someone who would later be involved at almost every stage of moviemaking, it's significant that he was already determined to branch out. With a close friend, Don Devlin, he managed to sell a screenplay entitled *Thunder Island* (1963) to Twentieth Century-Fox's B-picture unit — a script, moreover, which they had written in just three weeks. Since speed was essential to any dealings with Roger Corman and other traders in what might be called, after fast food, 'fast cinema', he became a 'short-order' scriptwriter.

Thunder Island was directed by Jack Leewood and starred Gene Nelson, Fay Spain and Brian

Kelly. It centered around the hiring by a group of Latin American militants of a loutishly callous killer (Nelson) for the purpose of assassinating an exiled dictator living in well-guarded isolation on an island off the coast of Puerto Rica. After the reluctant involvement of a disillusioned American businessman and his wife, and an abortive raid on the ex-President's luxuriously appointed villa, the movie ends abruptly and violently with the deaths of the hit-man and his beautiful accomplice. Though it would be a mite pretentious to call such a routine action programme 'prophetic', it's worth noting that Nicholson and Devlin had chosen the then unmodish theme of political assassination only a few months before John Kennedy's fatal visit to Dallas. Though the movie was weakest when it glibly attempted to add the gilt (or guilt) of contemporary relevance to the gingerbread of a servicable thriller plot, Jack's scripting début was warmly commended by both *Variety* and the British Film Institute's *Monthly Film Bulletin*. In general, he hadn't received such positive press notices since his performance in *Cry Baby Killer*.

In early 1964, he returned to acting — and, for the first time in his career, in a movie produced by a major studio. Joshua Logan's *Ensign Pulver* was a sequel to the much better known *Mister Roberts*, originally a novel and Pulitzer Prize-

J.N.'s scripting début, *Thunder Island*, **with Gene Nelson and Fay Spain**

winning Broadway play by Thomas Heggen, **then a** Warners movie co-directed by John Ford **and** Mervyn LeRoy with a cast including James **Cagney**, Henry Fonda and Jack Lemmon. Lem-**mon** played Ensign Pulver in the original and the **sequel** made Ensign Pulver a lemon. With **Roberts** dead at the end of the movie bearing his **name**, Burl Ives appropriated the role of the mar-**tinet** Captain and young Robert Walker Jnr was **cast** in the title role of the wheeler-dealer, womanizing ensign who endeavors to boost morale on board a forlorn USN vessel stationed in the Pacific in World War II.

Unfortunately, where *Mister Roberts* had managed to tread a poignant line between comedy and drama, *Pulver* soon ran aground on exhausting below-decks farce and inane desert island fantasies. And Jack Nicholson? Well, if you paid attention throughout, you might have glimpsed him as a crew member popping up beside rock singer Tommy Sands, the sourly good-natured Walter Matthau and a mildly overweight James Coco. He was unbilled in the credits, and possibly preferred it that way. The movie's sole connection with the real thrust of his career was the appearance of Millie Perkins, an acting school classmate who was to co-star with him in two Monte Hellman Westerns, *The Shooting* and *Ride in the Whirlwind*.

Though little appreciated in their country of origin, these twin movies have enjoyed enormous prestige in Europe, even winning several Festival awards. But Jack's long and fruitful partnership with Hellman started in less auspicious circumstances. For the same Fox B-picture unit that financed *Thunder Island*, they left together for Manila in 1964 to shoot *Back Door to Hell*, an undistinguished World War II programmer. Jack played one of three GIs (the others being Jimmie Rodgers and John Hackett) parachuted into the Philippine Islands on a reconnaissance mission to determine the strength and disposition of the Japanese forces prior to the US invasion. They swiftly make contact with local guerrilla leaders; and when the enemy threatens in retaliation to slaughter the children of a nearby village, they infiltrate Japanese headquarters, engage them in battle and finally succeed in transmitting crucial information to the American army. Though the action sequences, particularly the raid on the Japanese camp, were staged with conviction, and the native characters and settings benefited from Hellman's sharp eye for location, the movie spent too much of its relatively brief running time striving to counterpoint its facile gung-ho heroics with a modicum of antiwar sentiments, an endeavor undermined by the labored, derivative script. Nicholson re-

mained undistinguished from the other two leads; if questioned back in 1964 which of the trio possessed the greatest star potential, there is absolutely no guarantee that Jack would have been one's automatic choice.

Flight to Fury (1966), which was also filmed by Hellman in Manila, starred Dewey Martin, Fay Spain, Vic Diaz and Nicholson, who doubled as co-scenarist with its producer Fred Roos. The movie, however, was released only in 1968, before ending where it should have begun — as television fodder. The plot involved Jack as a stumblebum psychopathic killer in murderous pursuit of a cache of diamonds in the Far East. After his plane crashes in the jungle, he and his entourage squabble over the spoils, with the wholly predictable result that none of them lives to profit by their crimes. What is astonishing about such an abject pair of potboilers is that just twelve months later Hellman and Nicholson would collaborate on two of the most significant, most original Westerns of the last twenty years.

The Shooting, at a cost of 75,000 dollars, was co-produced by Nicholson and written, under the pseudonym of Adrien Joyce, by Carole Eastman, another friend from acting classes. Her brother Charles figured in the cast, which was headed by Warren Oates, Millie Perkins and Nicholson. Its narrative, ambiguous and allusive, doesn't lend itself to any easy summarizing. A former bounty hunter, Willet Gashade (Oates) deliberately leaves a trail for an unseen pursuer as he journeys with provisions to the isolated mine which he works with his brother and two friends. The death of one of his friends is revealed by a makeshift tombstone on a freshly dug grave, while the other, half-crazed, tells him that his brother (bearing the very un-American name of Coigne) has run amok since killing a man and child in a small township. They are subsequently joined by a mysterious woman (Perkins) and a sadistic hired gunman dressed in black, Jimmy Spear (Nicholson), who offer Gashade a large sum if he will escort them across the desert. On finally reaching their destination, the unnamed woman spies the man she has been seeking. While she is taking aim, a shot rings out. As both woman and bounty hunter fall to the ground, Gashade calls out the name of her adversary — 'Coigne!'. The screen fades to white.

Such spartan telegraphese hardly does justice to the starkly poetic textures and indefinable malaise with which this film is informed from its first image to the enigmatic stop-motion sequence of the climatic gunfight, over whose precise meaning more than one critic has pondered. (Does the woman kill Coigne? Does

J.N. closing his eyes to Burl Ives in *Ensign Pulver*

"...an undistinguished World War II quickie..." J.N. and John Hackett in *Back Door to Hell*

The Shooting

Coigne kill her, or his brother, or both? Are Coigne and the brother one and the same person?) Unusual for a Western, however frugally produced, is the tiny cast, the absence of any sense of civilization, of community, of *others*. Since there is nothing to distract from the central situation, the desert which they cross, unlike any other in the American cinema, becomes almost a symbolic space, a desert in more than the geographical sense. Each of the characters is a friendless loner — as witness one exchange: 'Did you ever leave behind a friend?' 'I never did have one' — and each seems to be at the end of his tether (or noose). Though one wouldn't care to make too much (as did certain extravagant French critics) of the plot's allegorical subtext, it's hard to rid oneself of the impression that this tale has been told many times before, perhaps in other, non-Western guises (the myth of Orpheus and Eurydice is only the most immediately apparent). At the same time, much of the movie's tension is generated by the way it fuses such symbolism with allusions to current media iconography. The jerky shootout, for instance, was quite conciously modeled on the celebrated newsreel footage of Jack Ruby gunning down Lee Harvey Oswald in the underground walkway of a Dallas police station.

Though *The Shooting* was not widely distributed in the States, and Jack's total earnings from it amounted to a princely 700 dollars, the acclaim it won from numerous European critics was undoubtedly instrumental in fostering a reputation (as yet only underground) for both actor and director. For the first time in his career, Jack's menacing presence seemed to prefigure a real star mythology — a phenomenon of which he himself must have been obscurely aware, since he agreed to tote the film in hatboxes to Cannes, Edinburgh and various other European film festivals. After years of passing unnoticed as just another leather-jacketed punk, he suddenly seemed a much more complex figure, elusive, amoral, sinister yet seductive, manly yet obsessed with some obscure, unformulated inadequacy, the stubble on his jawline signaling an anti-establishment stance rather than mere dishevelment. The time was approaching when critics would no longer consult their publicity handouts on leaving a press show to note which striking young actor had played a particular role, but would check in advance to see what role Jack Nicholson would be playing.

He and Hellman followed *The Shooting* with a second off-center Western, *Ride in the Whirlwind* (or, as it is sometimes titled, *Ride the Whirlwind*), 'a McLuhan mystery' which also starred Cameron Mitchell and Millie Perkins. Here Jack played a ranch cowboy, Wesp, forced to aban-

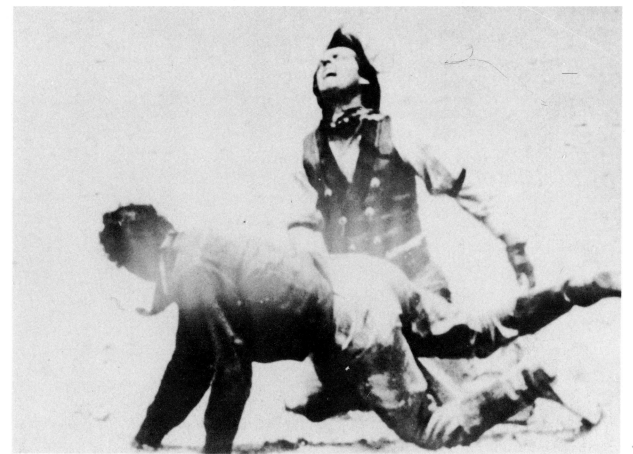

The Shooting

don his home in the company of a friend, Vern (Mitchell), because they are being pursued by an unseen character rather portentously named Cain. Nicholson, who once again doubled as co-scenarist, never offers the slightest clue as to the identity of this Cain or the reasons for his unrelenting pursuit of the two protagonists. Such wilful disregard for a basic narrative convention has consigned *Ride in the Whirlwind* to a deeper, even more nebulous limbo than its companion piece (they were shot almost simultaneously in the Utah Desert, with the same crew and some of the same cast). Deemed too stark and original for the attention span of a typical drive-in audience, it has never received proper distribution in America. Even in the UK where the director has many loquacious admirers among the critical fraternitiy, it is yet to be released. This conspiracy of silence appears to have taken Hellman by surprise. He is quoted as saying, 'We thought they would be a couple more Roger Corman movies that would play on the second half of a double bill somewhere. So any thoughts of doing something different were for our own personal satisfaction. We never thought that anybody would ever notice.'

But while the artistic intransigence of these works have tended to stunt the commercial potential of Hellman, who has been abandoned by or escaped from a number of mainstream pro-

jects, they helped to establish Nicholson as the American cinema's most quixotic loner, both attracted to and fastidiously repelled by the concept of the group. In *Whirlwind*, his character was diametrically opposed to the Hell's Angel-out-West, so to speak, that he personified in *The Shooting*. The role of Wesp offered him a chance of reprising his boy-next-door persona, sociable, polite and, notwithstanding the actor's age, ineradicably adolescent. While their odyssey across the sun-baked desert is perceived by Vern as banishment from the Edenic ranch which they ran together in harmony, Wesp is only at home in exile: in him may be detected that wanderlust which in American mythology finds its resolution in a westward movement. Though Vern's nostalgia is firmly rooted in the past, his past, his hearth and home, Wesp's emerges as a more abstract yearning for some natural, unsullied existence which can only be exorcised by endless wandering.

Jack was and has remained understandably proud of these two movies, in which his involvement was scarcely less creative than that of the director himself. Interviewed for the trade paper *Entertainment World* in 1969, he remarked without undue modesty: 'Not a single other human being could have made those films at that price, costumed at Western Costumes, 35mm, color. I did it by doing everything myself. Monte

Hellman, my former partner, cut it; I assisted. Monte directed; we co-produced. I played a part in each picture. We had short crews, worked long hours. People did favors. But you can't expect them to do favors forever.'

He never stopped working now, movie after movie. When he wasn't working at work, he worked at home. On scripts, on ideas for scripts (one of which was later to emerge as a *succès de scandale* for Roger Corman, *The Trip*). Inevitably, the marriage suffered. Sandra had been relegated to a supporting role in his life, and must sometimes have felt like an extra. A major problem was that, when she and Jack first met, they were both struggling unknowns, whose commitment to their work and to each other was equal. Now Sandra, who had withdrawn from acting to raise their child, represented the past for her husband, a by-product of whose increasingly Hollywoodized lifestyle was the proximity of beautiful, accommodating girls. Marriage and parenthood had come to seem almost an anomaly. Another problem arose when, as part of research undergone for the writing of *The Trip*, Jack judged it necessary to experiment with LSD, a practice abhorred by Sandra. In 1967 they divorced — quite amicably, with Jack continuing to pay frequent visits to Sandra and Jennifer, their daughter.

As had occured more than once before, however, his career took another vertiginous plunge on the rollercoaster after the twin peaks of *The Shooting* and *Ride in the Whirlwind*. *Hell's Angels on Wheels* (1967) need not detain one too long (and, given that Hell's Angels are, virtually by definition, 'on wheels', nothing can better expose the tired, secondhand nature of the whole project than this redundancy in its title). It was directed by Richard Rush, whose trademark would appear to be letting the sun dazzle the camera lens on every conceivable occasion, and featured Adam Roarke, Sabrina Scharf and Nicholson. Dealing with the involvement of a hick town garage attendant named 'Poet' (Nicholson) with a gang of rampaging motorcyclists, it was a carbon copy of every other movie on the subject, and the carbon had become pretty pallid. Where it was reviewed at all, it was demolished. *Variety* neatly summed up Nicholson's characterization as 'variations on a grin'.

Though Corman's *The St. Valentine's Day Massacre* (also 1967), which followed it, was an infinitely more polished movie, Jack's role was so negligible that it has sometimes been omitted from his filmography. Chicago 1928 — where violin cases were used for machine guns,

Ride in the Whirlwind with **Cameron Mitchell**

garages for massacres and bathtubs for gin, where genial, prosperous racketeers in double-breasted suits and Homburg hats, family men all, held board meetings in penthouse offices while, far below, their henchmen rubbed each other out in abandoned city lots. Corman's vivid recreation of the period was epitomized by some superb setpieces: the murder of a hoodlum in a florist's shop, bright scarlet blood welling out of three brand new pores in his body as he collapses senseless onto a funeral wreath (a graphic visual equivalence of the notion of 'liquidation'); a plushy restaurant reduced to rubble in a matter of minutes as a procession of hearse-like limousines briefly halts in front of its window to release a hail of bullets; the Massacre itself, Capone's poisoned Valentine to the rival Moran gang, with a whimpering dog holding a lonely wake over the seven riddled corpses. More tightly controlled than Corman's usual output, its semi-documentary ambitions, implied in the commentary (which begins 'A factual rendition of the events leading up to . . . '), tended to frustrate his penchant for inventively horrific imagery. But with impeccable performances from Jason Robards (as Al Capone), Ralph Meeker (as Bugs Moran), George Segal, and such dependable supporting actors as Frank Silvers, Bruce Dern and Harold J. Stone, it deserved its solid box-office success.

Nicholson was actually offered Dern's role but turned it down if favour of playing the driver of the getaway car, which provided him with three weeks work, an excellent salary and very little to do. In fact, Jack's single line of dialogue provided a somewhat humorless movie with its only amusing moment. One of the killers, in the process of greasing his revolver bullets, is asked by another 'What the hell are you doing?' Before he can reply, Nicholson chimes in with that inimitable growl of his, 'It's garlic. The bullets don't kill ya, ya die of blood poisoning!'

At the end of the same year, Corman was ready to film Jack's script, *The Trip* — though, to the scenarist's chagrin, he was passed over for the role he had mentally cast himself in, that of a drug 'guru' eventually played by Bruce Dern. The movie's protagonist is Paul Groves (Peter Fonda), a successful director of television commercials who, dissatisfied with his work and on the point of divorcing his wife Sally (Susan Strasberg), decides to experiment with LSD in a last desperate attempt to make some sense out of his life. Initially, under the omniscient supervision of an experienced friend John (Dern), his hallucinations are calm and soothing, even gently erotic — comprising intermingled images of Sally and a blonde beauty named Glenn (Salli

Sachse). Later, however, the trip goes sour: he imagines himself tortured, pursued, buried alive, then summoned before a phantasmagoric tribunal presided over by another friend Max (Dennis Hopper in his element), to whom he tries to justify the empty waste of his existence. Believing that he has killed John, the dazed Paul rushes out of the house and into a series of bizarre encounters on the L.A. streets, a discothèque, a laundromat and a café. Finally, he is led back to home and safety by Glenn, for whom he confesses his love the following morning. And that, I'm afraid, is all there is to Jack Nicholson's first solo effort at screenwriting.

There are so many problems with *The Trip* — a movie which has been variously admired, detested and ridiculed — that it's a delicate business just determining where to begin. But one might mention, for starters, the curious (and intended?) resemblance between the vapid TV commercial being set up by Fonda in the opening scene — a windblown couple embracing on a lonely Pacific beach to the accompaniment of an offscreen voice purring 'Anything is possible when you use April in Paris perfume' — and the garish psychedelic visions to which, under the influence of the drug, he subjects himself and which presumably inspire him to a higher understanding of his predicament (as also to a somewhat rash declaration of love). If a comparison is intended, if Corman is suggesting that drug-induced beatification can be as transitory and mindless as the ersatz bliss of a TV commercial, one queries the wisdom of devoting two-thirds of his movie's running time to ramming home such a basic argument. If not, then one can only state that the kaleidoscope of images which he allows the spectator to share with Fonda remains obstinately unconvincing as a glimpse beyond the twin portals of Heaven and Hell. Hallucinations are, in any event, notoriously tricky to depict on the screen, whether provoked by religious or pharmaceutical (or even Dharma-ceutical) ecstasy. Corman's meretricious barrage of optical effects, stroboscopic lighting, color filters, body painting, jump cuts, flashbacks and flash-forwards, not to mention the heavy throb of a human heart on the soundtrack, is more redolent of disco electronics than of any genuinely enlarged conciousness. When it's all over, Fonda's newly acquired eighth sense tends to find verbal expression in the same monosyllabic incoherence (he says 'Like... wow!' a lot) that characterized his reactions during the trip itself. As a response to Glenn's inquiry, 'Did you find what you were looking for? The insight?', all he can manage to articulate is 'Yeah, I think... like, I love you.'

Of marginally more interest (at least to indefatigable Corman-watchers) is the way in which the central section enables the director once more to parade the macabre obsessions familiar from his horror movies: the vaulted crypt in which Fonda is suspended upside down by his imaginary tormentors, the open grave in which he is prepared for premature burial, the tangled fairy-tale forest through which he is pursued by a horde of horsemen in black. But the script is, in the wrong sense, minimalist, the performances perfunctory, and the movie more conducive to giggles than awe.

At the time, however, it caused quite a stir. One reviewer compared it to Fellini's 8½ (though the figure might more accurately denote the movie's I.Q.), another confidently described it as Corman's best work (a greater compliment than many crabbed critics would still be willing to concede). Refused a release certificate by the British censor for several years (allegedly on the advise of a brace of psychologists), it was premièred in the UK during a Forbidden Film Festival. Four years later, when finally granted limited club distribution, it had nevertheless to carry a health warning like a pack of cigarettes. Both screenwriter and director dabbled with LSD themselves in order to obtain an insider's knowledge of its hallucogenic processes, and Jack described his experience thus: 'The psychiatrist blindfolded me for the first five hours. I regressed, re-experienced my own birth, was in the womb. It's hard to verbalize this kind of thing. I was an infant thinking I was wetting myself and talking with a small voice. I even felt like I was going to die. The doctor said, "Let yourself go." I did. I died. It was liberating. Then my wife came to get me. I mixed her up with my mother. And all the while I'm schizo and could look at myself. And was going with it. The old actor training. Go with it.'

Though *Psych-Out* (1968) was neither Richard Rush's Corman-produced nor directed, it did bear a family resemblance to *The Trip* — less by virtue of its subject matter than the presence of Nicholson, Strasberg and Dern in the cast. It was intended as a satirical portrait of the Haight-Ashbury community in the Sixties, in which drugs formed only one ingredient of an already timeworn iconography that also encompassed rock music (noisily performed on the soundtrack by such ephemeral groups as The Storybook, The Seeds and The Strawberry Alarm Clock) and the whole hippie and Flower Power subculture. Strasberg played a deaf seventeen-year-old come to bohemian San Francisco in search of her elder brother (Dern offering his familiar impersonation of a haunted acid-head).

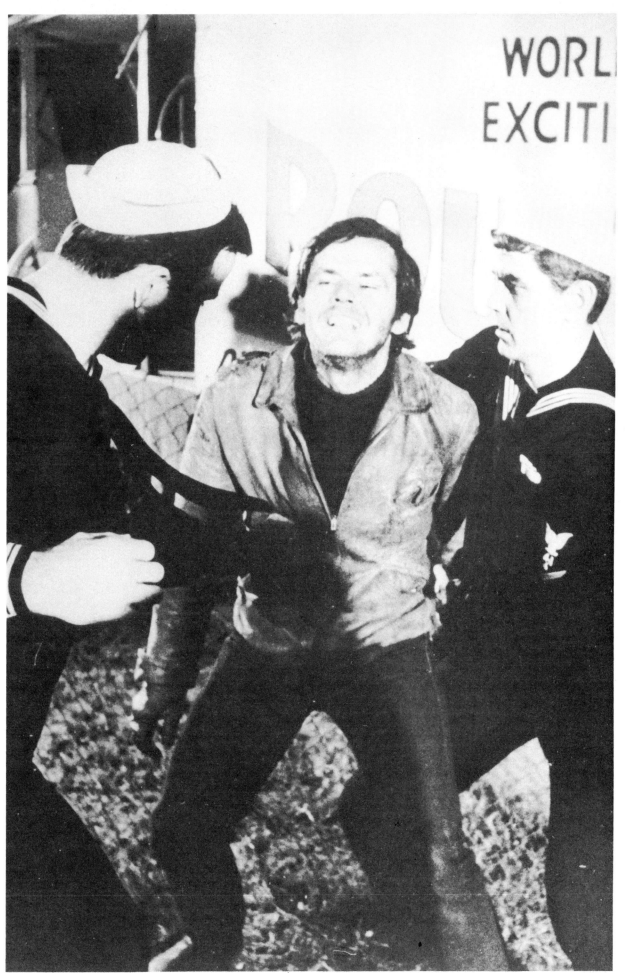

WORL
EXCITI

Just one of J.N.'s "variations on a grin" in *Hells Angels on Wheels*

Chicago 1928 *The St. Valentine's Day Massacre*

With the aid of four of his friends (Nicholson, Dean Stockwell, Adam Roarke and Max Julien), all of them musicians in a down-at-the-heel rock group, she discovers his whereabouts just as she begins to suffer the effects of a horrendously bad trip from a powerful hallucinogen. It all ends with a peculiarly San Francisco-like apocalypse, Strasberg wandering helpless between the traffic lanes on the Golden Gate bridge, one of the group struck down by an automobile while trying to carry her to safety, and Dern treating his own self-immolation as the ultimate 'trip'.

Rush's attempt to cross the wires of two very distinct genres, the Western and the hippie 'youth movie' resulted only in a short-circuit. A few of the visions assailing Strasberg in her climactic trip were diverting enough — alley walls gushing vapors and exploding into purple flames — without ever relating organically to the flatfooted pacing of the more naturalistic sequences. Nicholson, who played Stoney, one of the rock group, had to contend with the totally unfocused, underscripted characterization of a nervy hipster with a lean and hungry look. One could even sense a faint edge of desperation in his playing, as if he were starting to wonder whether he would be typecast till the end of his days. Of exclusively gossip-column interest was the presence, way down the cast list, of one I.J. Jefferson, aka Mimi Machu, the woman who was to be his companion in a stormy relationship for some years after his divorce.

If Jack had done more than merely muse about the possibility of opting out of the movies altogether, his biography would have to end right here (except, of course, that if *Psych Out* really had been his last film, no biography would ever have been written). Not that he had lost faith in his own abilities: it was Hollywood's capacity for usefully exploiting them that he had come to question. Apart from Hellman's pair of Westerns, which had remained almost unseen in the States, and *The Trip*, his script for which had been ignored by the critics, his career so far was not notably different from those of any number of long-suffering Hollywood hopefuls.

Yet prosperity was just around the corner — not only prosperity but celebrity, of the superstar brand. Before it all happened with *Easy Rider*, however, another movie was released which he scripted and in which he made a brief, unheralded appearance: *Head* (1968). Halfway between *Hair* and *Help!*, *Head* consisted of a series of extravagantly Surrealist vignettes as little related to each other as are the fleeting spasms which one catches of cops-and-robbers series, Westerns, old movies, talk shows and sports events when idly switching TV channels. With fellow-director James Frawley, Bob Rafelson had more or less invented the Monkees pop quartet for the purposes of a successful television sitcom. In this movie, their valedictory appearance, he was honest and witty enough to admit (even to flaunt the fact) that his four moppety marionettes — Micky Dolenz, David Jones, Mike Nesmith and Peter Tork — had originated as a gimmick before turning into a hit-parade pop group. In other words, to reverse the old cliché, if the Monkees hadn't been invented, they would never have existed. *Head* was their apotheosis, a film literally about nothing at all, its heroes creating the impression of having stuck their own heads through four holes in the screen, as in those fairground booths where one can be photographed as a boxer or a toreador.

All one can do to convey even a faint notion of the film's mood is cite a few random examples of its off-beat humor (a straightforward, linear synopsis is out of the question). A half-dozen of the cast credits read backwards on the screen. Others include heavyweight champion Sonny Liston as a movie extra, Frank Zappa as a critic, one Vito Scotti as 'I Vitelloni', T.C. Jones as both 'Mr and Mrs Ace', William Bagdad as 'Black Sheik' (or could that be Black Sheik as 'William Bagdad'?), Jack's friend I.J. Jefferson as 'Lady Pleasure' and Jack himself with Rafelson as 'themselves'. Victor Mature also appears, first seen camping it up in a TV commercial for which the Monkees are hired to 'play' the dandruff in his hair. At another point the boys find themselves transported into an archetypical Cavalry-and-Indian confrontation, until Mickey Dolenz summarily declares to an invisible presence just behind the camera, 'Bob, I'm through with it!' and stalks off. It all ends — and why not? — with the Monkees being hauled away in an immense glass tank. Of the frenetic non sequiturs that punctuate the movie, Frawley has commented, 'It was true surrealism, but of a very American style, bacause American surrealism is funny.' By 'American surrealism' Frawley was undoubtedly alluding to that strain of vaudeville-inspired lunacy which can be traced from *Hellzapoppin'* and the Marx Brothers right up to Mel Brooks and Co.

Renata Adler termed Nicholson's scattershot (indeed, scatterbrained) screenplay 'dreadful', which rather misses the point. To be sure, it lacks both character psychology and development, adopts (quite consciously) a hit-or-miss attitude towards its random succession of episodes and is as bereft of genuine personality as the four wind-up dolls it enshrines (and who were chosen, according to Rafelson, as deliberate pop group stereotypes: a tall, skinny one; a pretty, curly-

Four wise Monkees in *Head*

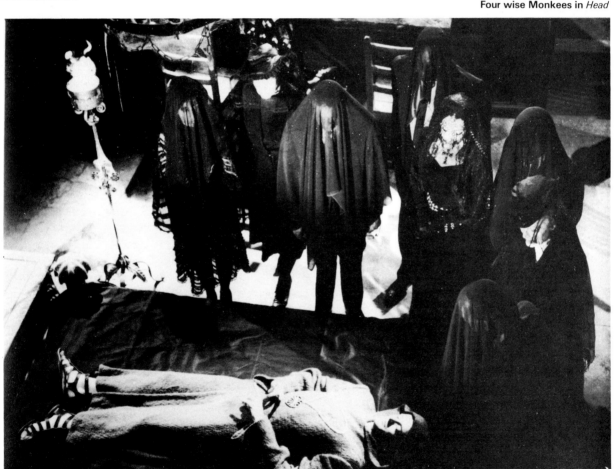

Peter Fonda's premature burial in *The Trip*

haired one; a goofy one; and a manic one). But it draws its inspiration, like the movie itself, from such discredited cultural artefacts as billboards, TV commercials, record covers, and the addle-pated lyrics of pot-influenced rock songs. In fact, *Head* possesses its own built-in defense mechanism to confound potential critics. If one complains that it doesn't make too much sense, the movie coolly ripostes that it isn't supposed to make sense; if one grumbles that it isn't con-sistently funny, one soon learns that it isn't sup-posed to be all that funny, and therein lies the real joke; if one remarks that the four pro-tagonists seem (except to the least dis-criminating of teeny boppers) almost identical, well, Nicholson and Rafelson have got there first. In one droll moment when — thanks to special ef-fects — the other three have mysteriously disap-peared from view, Nesmith, annoyed at finding himself alone in the frame, announces, 'If you think they call us plastic now, you wait till I get through telling 'em how we do it!'

"YOU KNOW, THIS USED TO BE HELL OF A GOOD COUNTRY."

The story behind *Easy Rider* (1969) — a movie which, however one feels about it, changed the face of American cinema — really begins with failure, the conspicuous failure in the late sixties of a few major studios to generate grosses for blockbuster productions commensurate with their budgets. The initial 'problem', so to speak, the trap into which they were prepared to walk blindfold, was Twentieth Century-Fox's immensely successful adaptation of the Rodgers and Hammerstein Broadway show, *The Sound of Music* (directed by Robert Wise in 1965), which became, and has remained, the most profitable musical in screen history. Though it seemed to offer conclusive proof that the movie public had an insatiably sweet tooth, the two points the Fox executives (and envious rivals at other studios) failed to realize were the degree to which its triumph had depended on a precise combination of circumstances, and that miracles (also known as packed houses) cannot easily be repeated. It wasn't only the presence, sickly yet bracing, of Julie Andrews at the height of her popularity, or the simpleminded but catchy melodies, or the breathtaking Alpine vistas of the Tyrol, it was all these together that had made the movie as tempting a prospect as a department store sale (and often a with similar clientèle). Fox's unhappy attempt to conjure up the same crowds for a second Wise musical,

Star! (1968, a biopic of Gertrude Lawrence with Julie Andrews yet again), demonstrated that even with an exclamation mark a star just wasn't enough. It was a disastrous flop, as were Richard Fleischer's *Doctor Dolitle* (1967, with Rex Harrison), which did indeed do little at the box-office, and Gene Kelly's *Hello Dolly* (1969, with Barbra Streisland and Walter Matthau).

Meanwhile Peter Fonda had approached Roger Corman with an idea for an inexpensive bike movie which he hoped to produce, with Dennis Hopper directing and Corman — in conjunction with a small but lively independent company, American International Pictures — as its executive producer. Since Samuel Z. Arkoff, the head of AIP, expressed serious doubts as to Hopper's capacity to bring the movie in on time, Nicholson suggested that it be transferred to Columbia via BBS, a new production company founded by Bob Rafelson, Bert Schneider and Steve Blauner, a proposal that brought him a tiny percentage of a movie which ended up grossing over 35,000,000 dollars. Yet he was only third choice for the role of George Hanson, one that would change his career as radically as *Easy Rider* changed the kind of movies to be produced in Hollywood for years to come. Rip Torn, who had originally been cast, fell out with Hopper and Fonda, Bruce Dern (whose progress as an actor had paralleled Nicholson's until

"...a deceptively laid back manner..." J.N.'s breakthrough performance in *Easy Rider*

precisely the success of this movie) demanded too high a fee. Third time lucky, then, for both film and performer.

Easy Rider deals with two young dropouts, Billy (Hopper) and Wyatt (Fonda), the latter nicknamed 'Captain America', who sell a large consignment of cocaine to a wealthy pusher near the Mexican border, stow the cash payment in Wyatt's fuel tank and set out across the country on their custom-built motorcycles (as Gilbert Adair points out in his *Vietnam on Film* 'the Harley-Davidson came to symbolize the period as, say, the Hispano-Suiza automobile had done for the Twenties'), the sole aim of their odyssey being to reach New Orleans for the Mardi Gras celebrations. But their shoulder-length hair, hippie outfits and psychedelically daubed machines cause them to be refused by motels and attacked by a redneck lynching party. A weather-beaten commune in New Mexico where they spend a few days founders through its metropolitan ignorance of basic agricultural skills; their experiment with LSD in a New Orleans cemetery degenerates into a hideously bad trip; and they both fall victim to a passing truckdriver, who guns them down almost 'for fun'.

Just another bike movie, it might have been. But what turned it into *the* bike movie was also a once-in-a-lifetime combination of circumstances. There was the fact that the Harley-Davidsons themselves proved to be not just any motorcycles. As they traversed the luridly beautiful landscapes of the American Southwest (very well photographed by Laszlo Kovacs), with their riders hunched over the handlebars in a position that looked to the layman both relaxed and uncomfortable, they became autonomous cinematic *forms*, as eligible for Hollywood's myth-making process as Ford's stagecoach in the Western to which it gave its title. The above-mentioned landscapes, too, had a significant *foreground* role to play: the two protagonists seemed to take pleasure from their beauty no less than, vicariously, did the spectator himself. As a metaphor for the country's pristine natural splendor before it was polluted by 'civilization', they evoked the near-hallucinatory visions of a 'trip' — one, paradoxically, in the literal sense. And whatever one's doubts as to the histrionic abilities of Peter Fonda and Dennis Hopper, they were ideally cast as *icons*, one a flaxen-haired, blue-eyed counterculture saint and martyr, a Don Quixote of peyotl, the other his incoherently stoned Sancho Panza.

What makes it difficult to align oneself with *Easy Rider*'s most ardent defenders, however, is its lack of authorial focus. Not everyone will be able to swallow it whole as an indictment of America's moral bankruptcy when Billy and Wyatt have contributed to the nation's potential for violence by dealing in the hardest of drugs in the first place. Are we supposed to wash our hands of that grubby prologue as cavalierly as the two heroes do? Is the boozy small town bigotry which they encounter *en route* with monotonous regularity really any worse, any more 'immoral', than selling cocaine, even if the proceeds from the latter are intended to finance a blissfully free-wheeling See-America-First pilgrimage? At one point Hanson, the Nicholson character, comments with wry melancholy, 'You know, this used to be a hell of a good country. I can't understand what's gone wrong with it.' But would the country in its supposedly halcyon past have any more readily tolerated such anti-social misfits? The movie never comes to terms, let alone grips, with these contradictions, which means that it ends up preaching — and it is a rather preachy work — to the converted.

Though critical reactions were mostly positive, there was an ecstatic unanimity where Nicholson's performance was concerned. In view of his current eminence, it's no longer very easy to understand how strongly original his touching, tragicomic characterization must have appeared to critcs at the time — critics, after all, who could barely have remembered him from previous roles. Which is why, though he had 'been around' for more years than he cared to think about, this appearance was treated as an overnight sensation, a revelation. Vincent Canby's lyrical notice in the *New York Times* was typical of the paeans of praise that suddenly to fell his lot: 'As played by Nicholson, George Hanson is a marvelously realized character, who talks in a high squeaky Southern accent and uses a phrase like 'Lord have mercy' the way another man might use a four-letter word. (. . .) There is joy and humor and sweetness when he smokes grass for the first time and expounds on the elaborate theory as to how the Venutians have already conquered the world.'

Where Fonda and Hopper could only muster that pop-up poster flatness peculiar to icons, one felt one could walk around Hanson and view him from different, even diametrically opposed, angles. He impressed as having a past that stretched beyond the boundaries imposed by the movie's narrative. He never postured (unlike Fonda in particular), adopted a deceptively laid back manner with such lazy, good-natured elegance that one was persuaded the camera had merely to start running in front of him and a performance would unfold. Though he was the bearer of the film's hamfisted ideological

J.N. initiated into "the splendours and miseries of marijuana"

'message', he remained detatched from its singlemindedness: in other words, whereas Bobby and Wyatt were inextricably bound up with everything that *Easy Rider* was trying to convey, Hanson, perched on Wyatt's bike in an old seersucker jacket and football helmet, seemed genuinely to have crossed their path by chance. He might as easily have turned up in quite another movie.

During the shooting of *Easy Rider*, cast and crew had a series of adventures only slightly less picturesque than those depicted onscreen. The campfire sequence, for example, when Billy and Wyatt initiate Hanson into the secrets of marijuana, required Nicholson to smoke what even for him was an inordinate number of joints — by some unlikely accounts, 155! Whatever the count, it may explain why this 'privileged moment' managed to capture the euphoria of the drug experience far more vividly than the whole of *The Trip*'s multimedia assault on the spectator's sensibilities. On another occasion, he and Hopper set off on an expedition to where D.H. Lawrence was buried in Taos, New Mexico. Hopper, who reported how they stretched out together on top of his grave, omitted to mention whether they could feel the English novelist spinning inside it. Ironically, though they were based for part of the time in a hamlet identical to those portrayed in the movie with such venom, since they were 'film stars' only *pretending* to be long-haired dropouts, they were welcomed by the locals with open arms.

Jack won the New York Film Critics Award for his performance, and to their collective astonishment sent polite thank-you notes to each and every one of them. He was, as they say, 'hot'. So, for the first time, he was offered a role in a major studio project by a distinguished director. Years later, interviewed about his cameo appearance in Ken Russell's *Tommy* (1975), Nicholson caustically referred to this work: 'I did sing once before in an epic that shall be nameless but they had the good sense to leave me on the cutting room floor. Let me say at least I sing better than Oliver Reed (also in *Tommy*). I'm available for touring next season. All the American record companies are in the hands of friends of mine but not one of them has signed me up yet. I guess that's self-critical enough.' The epic he was alluding to cayly was *On a Clear Day You Can See Forever* (1970), directed by the veteran Vincente Minnelli.

On a Clear Day originated as a Broadway musical by Burton Lane and Alan Jay Lerner; then, as with many a Broadway musical before it (*Brigadoon*, *Kismet*, *Bells Are Ringing*), Minnelli was assigned to turn it into an archetypical

2.10 - 10 - 66

With Barbra Streisand in *On a Clear Day You Can See Forever*

MGM movie musical. Even if in this instance the studio involved was Paramount, it remained an MGM musical in spirit. Barbra Streisand played Daisy Gamble, a mild and mousy Brooklyn girl who is desperately eager to give up chain-smoking for the sake of her staid but ambitious fiancé (Larry Blyden). After gatecrashing a lecture on hypnotism given by an ultra-suave French psychiatrist (Yves Montand), she makes the startling discovery that she is capable of succumbing to his powers at the slightest provocation; even more unexpectedly, she finds herself, under hypnosis, mentally transplanted to nineteenth century England as a beautiful adventuress named Melinda. The doctor, of course, is soon smitten with his exceptionally intriguing and cooperative patient (or rather with her earlier, more glamorous incarnation); but though they can't be united in the movie's own time span, all *will* end happily ever after in the twenty-first century where, according to Daisy's extrasensory perception, they are destined to meet yet again.

Since one of Minnelli's recurring thematic obsessions has been the opposition between fantasy and reality, theater and life, role-playing both in and out of the limelight, he was temperamentally suited to such fey material. And, indeed, there is much to enjoy here: a melodious score by Burton Lane; the exquisitely modulated visual contrast between the cool, sharp-edged present (Manhattan) and the lush, passionate past (Regency Brighton, designed in rich scarlets and golds by Cecil Beaton); the impeccable comic timing of Streisand in both roles, especially as, for once, she seems to have restrained her notorious megalomania and doesn't run ramrod over her fellow performers. But the golden age of the musical was over, and one can detect — oddly for as extrovert a director as Minnelli — a certain reticence, as if those around him were actively struggling to play down the fact that the movie belonged to the genre at all. A pair of the original show's liveliest production numbers were pointlessly cut, and too many of those left in were denied the breathing space that would have allowed them to build properly. A Hollywood musical is a loud, confident entertainment or it is nothing, and what compromised *On a Clear Day You Can See Forever* was some fatal indecision at the conceptual stage.

In any event, it was marginal to Nicholson's career, and can most generously be regarded as an aberration. Since he had finally made his reputation with *Easy Rider*, a certified youth movie, it was only to be expected that mainstream Hollywood would cast him as a 'hippie'.

But Tad Pringle, the ludicrously named character he played, was very much a Hollywood hippie (as one talks of 'Beverly Hillbillies'). He appeared briefly (and uncomfortably) as Streisand's rich neighbor, sharing a dispensable exchange with her on a studio-recreated rooftop patio. To Rex Reed in the *New York Times* he described the experience with characteristic drollery: 'I didn't take a step in the whole thing after I walked in carrying my suitcase. From that moment on, I'm either leaning on a window with flowerpots or up against a chimney or something. Once he let me get up to light someone's cigarette and I think my back went crrac-cuncchh. You can probably hear it on the screen. There was so little, uh, movement, you know what I mean. I didn't have that much to do. You have to sort of guess what he (Minnelli) wants. One day I said, "Look, Vincente, I really don't mind being directed, you know what I mean?"' Since it was Nicholson's singing voice that had appealed to the director in the first place, the reason for editing out his solo number will forever remain one of Hollywood's less absorbing enigmas. Perhaps just as well.

A musical note of a very different kind was struck by *Five Easy Pieces*, which Bob Rafelson directed in 1970 for BBS Productions and which immediately set Jack's career back on the rails again — this time for good. It was a typical, even prototypical, product of the New Hollywood, emphasizing subjectivity, detachment, personal crises and, above all, the inadequacy of America's traditional values, artefacts and institutions. Though in no way a film *about* Vietnam, *Five Easy Pieces* is suffused with the troubled self-questioning and self-recrimination which tore the country apart for the period of the war and its aftermath. A figure who would have been portrayed as an eccentric misfit on the fringe of movies made only a decade earlier, Nicholson's Bobby Dupea, for which he won an Oscar nomination as Best Actor, became the American cinema's first true hero (*not* antihero — the times were with him) of the Seventies.

Dupea, the drifting offspring of a middle-class family of musicians, is first seen amid the oil rigs and construction sites on which he works in order to make some fast money. Two concurrent crises arise to shatter this congenial routine: his living companion, a red-haired waitress named Rayette (Karen Black), is pregnant and expects him to marry her, and his sister (Lois Smith) urges him to return home where his father is gravely ill. Unable to ditch Rayette, he parks her at a cheap motel near his home in Puget Sound, hoping that she might leave him altogether, then rediscovers the family routine of earnest discus-

J.N. and Maria Schneider working together "in a surprisingly likeable, easygoing fashion" in *The Passenger*

sions and endless sessions of classical music that presumably caused him to opt out in the first place. The gravity of his father's condition (he has been almost totally incapacitated by a stroke) and abrupt termination of a casual affair with his brother's fiancée (Susan Anspach), not to mention the nightmarishly ill-timed intrusion of the sluttish, working-class Rayette into the family enclave, end by driving Dupea out onto the road again. Stopping at a petrol station, he hands his wallet over to Rayette to buy some coffee; while she is idly waiting for the car's tank to be filled, he hitches a ride aboard a passing truck.

Though *Five Easy Pieces* was patently inspired by the example of a small-budget 'road movie' like *Easy Rider*, the differences between the two are no less evident than their similarities. Like Billy and Wyatt, Dupea both rejects and is rejected by the middle-American dream, exemplified here by raucous wife-swapping beer parties and couples who have to raise their children in tiny, cramped caravans illuminated by the hypnotic flicker of a TV screen. Like them, too, he is caught in a transient circuit of bars, motels and gas stations, never straying very far from the highways that zigzag across the country like so many rivers and their tributaries. But if the *Easy Rider* duo rode into the movie as fully grown icons silhouetted against the picturesque sunset of a declining civilization, possessing neither past nor future, the precise source of Dupea's restless peregrinations — the provincial complacency and intellectual aridity of a cultured middle-class background — is explored by Rafelson and screenwriter Adrien Joyce through a series of telling confrontations between himself and his family. This was a daring stroke, as the earthy vitality of the 'redneck' sequences in the first half are so beautifully observed, energetic and often funny that the movie might have coasted along quite entertainingly on them.

Another fundamental difference with *Easy Rider*'s counter-culture hagiography is its skeptical approach to Dupea himself. Billy and Wyatt were never questioned in their self-ordained roles as 'kings of the road', as the nation's last free spirits brought down in their prime by fascistic bigots who had betrayed America's promise. Dupea, on the other hand, is portrayed quite clearly by both actor and director as a social weakling who exploits the road as an escape route when those who gravitate around him begin to suffocate him with their emotional demands. (The truck into which he climbs at the end is headed for Alaska, the country's last frontier and in every sense 'the end of the road'.) Dupea's tragedy is his own uncomfortable

awareness of his predicament: to his stroke-ridden father he confesses, 'I move around a lot, not because I'm looking for anything, but to get away from things that go bad if I stay.' And the Susan Anspach character defends her brutal rejection of him in similar terms: 'Where would it lead? A man with no love for himself, no respect for himself, no love for friends, family, work, *anything* — how can he ask for love from someone else?' At least, in what Dupea contemptuously refers to as the 'rest home' of the house in Puget Sound, she has succeeded in mapping out a space for herself; his only desire is to move off the map altogether.

Dupea's alienation emerges as all the more subtle than that of Billy and Wyatt because it doesn't derive from objective factors which would, after all, alienate anyone with an atom of intelligence or sensibility. The most he has to contend with, in a hilarious, brilliantly played and written scene, is the rigid adherence to rules of a waitress in a roadside diner, from whom he makes a doomed attempt to order chicken minus the toasted sandwich which invariably accompanies it. (It was inspired by an incident involving Jack and witnessed by Carol Eastman. Confronted in a restaurant with just this kind of obtuseness, he had lost his cool and screamed at the waitress, 'You say one word and I'll kick in your pastry cart!') Dupea lives in a wholly recognizable world, devoid of the loaded sentimentality of disgust that marred much of *Easy Rider*, and the achievement of the movie is to have conjured up the anxieties of midcentury alienation without any special pleading.

A complex film (by Hollywood standards, at least), *Five Easy Pieces* demanded, and received, from Nicholson a correspondingly complex central performance. Perhaps because they were old friends, Rafelson drew from the actor levels of characterization that surprised even those who had already tipped him for stardom on the evidence of *Easy Rider*. Nicholson had initially refused to play the scene, considered by Rafelson as crucial to the character's psychology, where Dupea breaks down in front of his paralysed father. 'Jack said Dupea was crying out of self-pity — something Jack strongly opposed in himself and in others,' Rafelson recalls. 'I argued that Dupea was crying out of an agony of displeasure over the life he was leading, and that this displeasure had to be revealed. Finally, I said, "Jack, this is all bullshit. You don't want to do it because you can't.".' The following morning Rafelson ordered the set to be cleared and Nicholson needed only a single take to do the scene superbly. Later, he himself commented, 'I've

Five Easy Pieces

been asked dozens of times whether I was really thinking of my own father and his tragedy during that scene. The answer is, of course I was.'

Another difficult moment, the ending, went through numerous changes right up to the last week of shooting and became a point of contention between Jack and his co-star, Karen Black. The original script, approved by Black, had Dupea and Rayette going over a cliff in their automobile, with only Rayette surviving. Jack was in favor of an ending which would have had Dupea walking away down a lonely street, and neither he nor Rafelson cared much for the notion of the character's sudden, gratuitous death. Finally, as so often happens in the movie business, a compromise was reached, which is what we see on the screen.

To general surprise (and it still seems surprising today, given what a restrained, reflective mood piece it is), *Five Easy Pieces* was as successful commercially as critically. Since much of this success could be attributed to Nicholson's performance (he appears in virtually every scene), he was bombarded with offers. He was able to move into a grander house, though as ever its door was left unlocked for friends to wander in at will. He paid regular visits to the Manson trial ('I just wanted to see it for myself'), jotting down odd scribbled notes on the macabre proceedings, either for an eventual project (never realized) or just out of sheer human curiosity. It was at this time, too, that he began to build up an extraordinary collection of pig effigies: stuffed toy pigs, carved wooden pigs, a pig matchholder and a needlepoint which depicted a pair of pigs coupling. 'When pigs became the symbol of evil,' he explained to bemused visitors, 'I adopted them.' His stormy affair with Mimi Machu continued unabated, though every Sunday without fail he spent in the company of his daughter Jennifer. While sometimes cold and remote to newcomers, he remained faithful to all his old cronies from acting school days — even if he had already acquired a celebrity which was taking him professionally out of their league.

After one last hiccup in a smoothly running career (the belated release of an undistinguished 1967 programmer, *Rebel Rousers*, in which he had been cast yet again as a hip, streetwise delinquent and which had been dredged out of the vaults solely on the strength of Nicholson's name), his irresistible rise proceeded on cue. Eight years before, he had submitted Jeremy Larner's novel, *Drive, He Said*, to BBS as possible material for a movie adaptation. The production company had taken an option, but nothing happened until Jack himself had reached such a

secure position that they could afford to finance it if he were to direct. With Larner he collaborated on the screenplay; and in late 1970, prior to the release of either *On a Clear Day You Can See Forever* or *Five Easy Pieces*, the production finally got under way.

Some first films are made as if they were going to be the last. The young director crowds too many ideas into too restricted a narrative framework, forgets to grant his characters much scope for behavioral freedom beyond the immediate demands of the plot, and often adopts a showy, look-mom-no-hands attitude to visual style. The result is that the completed product is offbeat, overheated and ultimately unsuccessful. *Drive, He Said* is just such a movie. Where *Five Easy Pieces* managed to reflect the deep divisions of opinion over Vietnam without ever referring to the war by name, *Drive* endeavors to allegorize the national mood through the opposition of its two protagonists, an apolitical basketball champion and a freaked-out draft dodger. And where Rafelson's movie could accommodate in its rambling plotline such ostensibly irrelevant digressions as Dupea's tantrum in the diner or another droll scene in which he and Rayette pick up two oddball Lesbians, *Drive* sucks everything, both characters and incident, into its inexorable narrative progress. *Drive, He Said*: the phrase might also describe Nicholson's aggressive approach to film-making.

The story he has to tell concerns Hector (William Tepper) and Gabriel (Michael Margotta), the two friends mentioned above, and how Hector's growing disaffection from the 'healthy' athletic chauvinism of his college life runs parallel to the subversive activities of his roommate Gabriel, whose group of student 'guerrillas' take over the PA system and disrupt a major game (one which is receiving live TV coverage). Later, Gabriel receives his draft papers and embarks on a crash course of sleepless nights and heavy drug consumption to ensure his unfitness for military service, while Hector pursues an unsatisfactory love affair with his professor's wife, Olive (Karen Black). His game rapidly deteriorates, he rejects an offer to turn professional out of distaste for what he sees as the blatant commercialism of the big-league teams, and is finally abandoned by the pregnant Olive. The movie ends with Gabriel assaulting a psychiatrist at his Army medical, breaking into Olive's room and attempting to rape her, then freeing all the animals and reptiles in the university biology labs before being carted off in an ambulance.

To be sure, as much because Nicholson

Michael Margotta as "a freaked-out draft dodger" in *Drive, He Said*

J.N. practising *Five Easy Pieces* on the piano

himself is no humorless pedant as through the fidgety charm of his performers (who also include the excellent Bruce Dern as a bullish, latently homosexual basketball coach and Henry Jaglom, later to direct Jack in *A Safe Place*), *Drive, He Said* is considerably less schematic than this synopsis would suggest. The sports sequences in particular are filmed with such virtuosity of hand-held camera movement that they have their own refreshing energy distinct from any 'symbolic' role; and it's significant that, in a work which treats Gabriel's gestures of revolt as well-intentioned but futile and even cruel (as when he releases Olive's budgerigars to certain starvation in the forest), Hector's chronic indecision toward what he is seeking from life emerges as far more human and sympathetic. Nicholson, oddly, spoke about the movie with perhaps greater lucidity than he made it. To John Russell Taylor in *Sight and Sound*, he expressed a few of his doubts: 'At the time I didn't think the film would be commercial. There were already other college milieu films on the market, and though I felt certain I would make the best of them, I didn't think that would be enough. Also, I realized that if you have a drama with two central characters, neither of whom is totally right or totally wrong, and the interest is very evenly divided between them, you are breaking one of the first rules of

financing: the first thing anyone asks is, where's the rooting interest? (. . .) One of the things I like about the college film is that when people are naive and young, for me they have the license to *state* a philosophy; it never plays right with the older characters. If you're working with an academic community as a microcosm, it is more organically right that characters can speak dialogue with a more philosophical turn.'

Perhaps the problem with the movie is that its philosophy *is* baldly stated rather than woven into some rich narrative texture, and the college community is so busy serving as a microcosm that it has been given little opportunity to exist in its own right. But it was a promising début, all things considered, and hardly deserved the frosty reception accorded to it by the vast majority of American critics. At the 1971 Cannes Film Festival it was greeted with unqualified scorn: the audience of professionals, journalists and hangers-on hooted, whistled and waved indignant fists at poor Jack and his two leading actors, Tepper and Margotta, who had flown over for the screening. More predictably, he found himself engaged in what he described as a 'stand-up, knockdown fight' with the British censor, John Trevelyan, over the climax of an explicit lovemaking scene in which Karen Black is heard to moan, 'I'm coming.' In the States, the movie

J.N. wearing his director's cap for *Drive, He Said*

had initially been given an X-rating on account of its frontal nudity and the fact that a female character did not merely express her physical fulfillment in the expected (and authorized) monosyllabic murmurs, but actually confessed onscreen to having an orgasm. Though *Drive,* *He Said* was eventually released with an 'R', it transpired that it never had possessed the commercial potential which Nicholson believed would be compromised by an 'X', and it flopped nationwide. For the moment, he decided to move out of the driver's seat.

"FORGET IT, JAKE, IT'S CHINATOWN."

It was only at weekends that Jack was able to edit *Drive, He Said*, as on weekdays he was acting in Mike Nichol's *Carnal Knowledge* (1971). Scripted with an impeccable ear for idiom (and for idiomatically foul language) by the cartoonist, dramatist and chronicler of contemporary American angst, Jules Feiffer, it dealt with the erotic preoccupations of two young men, Jonathan (Nicholson) and Sandy (Art Garfunkel, the second half of Simon and Garfunkel), from college in the Forties to middleaged disillusionment in the Seventies. Each is what the other is not. Jonathan is a cynical, snake-eyed Lothario, a 'Priapic demon', as one critic defined him, whose resemblence to Mozart's Don Giovanni with his catalog of 1003 — 'mille e tre' — conquests is emphasized by the scene in which he details his own list in the form of a slide lecture to his appalled but spellbound friend. And Sandy, first seen as a forlorn wallflower at a college dance, develops into an aging conformist, humorless and moustachioed. The various women who cross their paths (and sometimes, disconcertingly, vanish from the movie for long stretches of its running time) are played by Candice Bergen, Ann-Margret, Rita Moreno, Cynthia O'Neal and Carol Kane. There are no other male characters of note.

Carnal Knowledge had a brilliant, eye-catching title of the instantly *legible* type in which writer-director Paul Shrader has since specialized (*Blue Collar*, *Hard Core*, *American Gigolo*), and it's interesting to speculate just how much of the movie's huge success derived from those two suggestive words on posters and marquees. It was also surprisingly successful in the way it handled the problem of a triple-period structure. The tracing of the characters' sexual anxiety as over the years it shifts almost imperceptibly into discontent was conveyed both through intelligent, affecting performances by everyone concerned and through Nichols' discreet stylization, matching each period to the type of movie then current (the Fifties treated as a softly lit romantic comedy, the following two decades accorded a free-wheeling, *nouvelle vague*-inspired looseness of texture). Finally, the modulation between comedy and drama, realized so coarsely in Nichols' earlier success *The Graduate*, was notable here for its subtlety, so that it became impossible to categorize the movie clearly in either of the two genres.

Less effective, however, was its episodic narrative line and chic knowingness, which doubtless derived from the witty but thin-textured doodles of Feiffer's cartoon strips. Though his dialogue was one of the film's sources of pleasure, he never really allowed the scenario to build to that single, unifying statement about sexual malaise which the spectator

J.N. acquiring *Carnal Knowledge* **of Ann-Margaret**

had been led all along to expect; and, perverse as it may be to say so, he was perhaps not the most apposite choice of screenwriter. It seems, too, a miscalculation to have permitted Candice Bergen's role to be so abruptly truncated; however poignant the other women are, Bergen was there first and one cannot help wondering for too long after her disappearance just what might have happened to her. The presence of Garfunkel's Sandy also becomes much less significant in the second half, where he is gradually transformed into a passive observer of Nicholson's male chauvinist pig sniffing out his delectable female truffles.

Though Nicholson's overly virtuoso performance was criticized in some quarters for unbalancing the movie (Julian Jebb complained in *Sight and Sound* that 'Nicholson drives his way through the film in a moral vacuum. His rages, like his worries about his potency, are finally uninteresting. Whether we see him as a psychotic or as a shit with problems, he remains a mannered actor giving a star performance'), it's possible to admire Nichols' judgment in juxtaposing what is indeed a star performance with the more ingenuous, more vulnerable characterizations of the actresses, few of whom had ever before been taken seriously in the cinema. Bergen, for example, is superlative as the touching but dangerously double-edged Susan, and Ann-Margret, hitherto a showgirl of dubious distinction, admirably captures sexual contentment in a lengthily held shot of her propped up on pillows beside Nicholson. *Carnal Knowledge* was an intelligent, adult movie whose box-office success was as merited as it was unsurprising. Less merited, though in a way equally unsurprising, was *Harvard Lampoon's* choice of Nicholson as Worst Actor of 1972 — along with Candice Bergen as Worst Actress (though in another movie, *T.R. Baskin*) and Stanley Kubrick's *A Clockwork Orange* as Worst Film.

An odd little incident occurred in Vancouver during the shooting of *Carnal Knowledge* that confirmed the extent to which the incidentals of Nicholson's performance were drawn from his own impulsive nature. He had been strolling in the woods and stopped at a country club where he requested a glass of water. When the barman, who evidently failed to recognize him, turned him down, Jack started screaming, 'Are you trying to tell me that as a human being you're refusing to give me a glass of water?' Shades of Bobby Dupea. . . as also of the crassly mercenary mores with which he was at odds in *Five Easy Pieces*.

Little space need be expended on Henry Jaglom's *A Safe Place* (1971), an indigestible mound of yesterday's lukewarm whimsy. One charitably assumes that Nicholson — who could, after all, afford to be discriminating in his choice of scripts — consented to play in it as a favor to Jaglom (an old friend who had appeared in *Drive, He Said*) and the production company, BBS. Since the movie proved incapable of telling its story coherently, synopsising it would be a pointless exercise: suffice to say that it centered on the winsome fantasies of Susan, sometimes called Noah (Tuesday Weld), and the unappetising collection of freaks by whom she is surrounded. These include Orson Welles as a jovial, pixilated magician, given to recounting excruciatingly gnomic anecdotes, such as the one beginning, 'Last night, in my sleep, I dreamed that I was sleeping, and dreaming in that sleep that I had awakened, I fell asleep. . .' Come again? Or rather, don't bother. There is Bari, a tearfully suicidal creature (played by Gwen Welles, Orson's niece), who confesses how she overcame her fears of the lustful stares directed at her by Bowery winos by simply joining them in their fantasies (a solution not to be recommended outside of the movies). There are also two suitors, the dullard Fred (Philip Proctor), who is framed by camera movements as sluggish as he is himself, and the mercurial, high-spirited Mitch (Nicholson), around whose sprightly form the camera circles endlessly, as if some frenzied dervish were whirling just offscreen. That happiness is something irrevocably lost with childhood and only to be recaptured through fantasy is a retrograde but appealing notion; but the Eden recaptured in *A Safe Place* is, also what's usually known as 'second childhood'. Jack seems rarely to have alluded to it since.

Of much greater importance was Rafelson's *The King of Marvin Gardens*, the first movie made by Nicholson in 1972. Though he could now command up to half a million dollars a performance, for his three months work with Rafelson he charged only the minimum laid down by the Screen Actors Guild. For him, as for everyone else connected with the project, it was a labor of love. It was almost as if he were aware even before shooting began that the film, though in the line of *Five Easy Pieces*, could not make a profit, even if to an interviewer he once expressed his dissatisfaction at how it had been 'packaged'. '*The King of Marvin Gardens* is essentially very Kafkaesque. Everyone knows Kafka, everyone pays lip service to him as a great writer. But he's not exactly a publishing item to make anybody rich. Now I honestly feel, to put it naively, that if I were Kafka's agent, or I published Kafka, I would have found some way to achieve some sort of proper remuneration for

J.N. as a ''priapic demon'' with Art Garfunkel in *Carnal Knowledge*

''...yesterday's lukewarm whimsy...'' J.N. with Tuesday Weld in *A Safe Place*

what he was and what his writings are.' He believed that to have withheld the film's release for six weeks in order that it might be premièred at the New York Festival was a bad commercial misjudgment, in that it immediately became labeled as an 'intellectual' work which needed the Festival slot to generate any excitement at all.

The King of Marvin Gardens is set in Atlantic City as it was before the current gambling boom: a world of peeling rose-pink rococo facades, of melancholy, windswept carnivals, its once proud hotels now serving as an elephant's graveyard for senior citizens, its elegant Boardwalk, once a rival to Nice's Promenade des Anglais, now given over to busloads of loud, camera-toting sightseers. To this city, caught between a glorious past and an as yet uncertain future, comes David Staebler (Nicholson), a frustrated novelist ('No one reads any more. I have been deprived of my literary right and I crave an audience') and the host of a late-late radio talk show, who has been summoned by his elder brother Jason (Bruce Dern). Jason, a front man for the black racketeer Lewis ('Scatman' Crothers), is the archetypical American hustler, whose current scheme is to purchase an island off the coast of Hawaii and turn it into a vacationer's paradise. Emotionally involved with this restless, footsore misfit still clinging to the illusion that the jackpot will one day ring out for him are Sally (Ellen Burstyn) and her sexily beautiful stepdaughter Jessica (Julia Anne Robinson). Like Monopoly pieces (the game's original American 'setting' is, of course, Atlantic City), they move aimlessly around the board, dream of constructing houses and hotels, 'go directly to jail' (Jason has been imprisoned on a felony charge trumped up by a suspicious Lewis, while David himself has spent a few months in a sanatorium), and all end up losers. During an acrimonious row between the two brothers, Sally becomes distraught at the prospect of being abandoned for Jessica. In an uncontrolled fit of hysteria, she suddenly shoots Jason, whose body David is left to transport back to Philadelphia where he returns to his confessional monologues on the air.

Nicholson's Staebler is a nocturnal creature, blinking behind his mild-rimmed glasses at the dazzling sunlight of the gaudy resort. He is first seen in a long, tortured close-up, his tic-ridden features framed in a tiny pool of light against the darkness. Addressing the camera, he hesitantly confides a memory of the day he and his brother deliberately allowed their grandfather, choking on a stray fishbone, to cough himself to death. Suddenly, a flashing red light reveals that he is in fact broadcasting this confession, dispensing morbid anecdotes and philosophical reflections to a ghostly public of insomniacs. Later, he sets off home through a labyrinth of shadowy streets, glass-and-steel office buildings, flights of stairs and subway corridors. A descent into hell, one senses — and yet, when he reaches home, his noisily but somehow healthily spluttering grandfather is there to meet him.

David, it's clear, has opted out, or rather opted *in* — into a private, hermetically sealed world from which all competition has been banished. But in the land of opportunity one cannot so easily escape one's inalienable, constitutional right to the pursuit of happiness — indeed, the movie goes so far as to suggest that it has become almost one's *duty*. The aptly named Atlantic City (which sounds as if it might have originated in some didactic science-fiction vision of America) is both the emblem of that ideology and its wreck. With buildings half-erected so that one cannot tell whether they are going up or coming down, nothing in this decaying playground ever seems to acquire permanence. In a poignant mixture of individual fantasy and its crassly mercenary exploitation, a Miss America pageant is held in a deserted Convention Hall with the aid of a solitary electrician, Sally at the massive Wurlitzer organ and Jessica as the sole contestant and therefore the winner. But that same mixture is achieved day after day in Atlantic City on a more humdrum level through the tired, fetishistic reiteration of the American Dream's crackerbarrel maxims: 'Tomorrow is another day', 'Another day, another dollar', 'The early bird catches the worm'. David and Jason are two sides of the same coin, one trying to turn reality into fantasy, the other almost managing to turn his fantasy into reality. Not so surprising, then, for their story to end where fantasy and reality meet, in death. An extra irony is reserved for the movie's coda — David's return to his nightly vigil over the radio waves. His show is titled 'Etcetera'; and, as the closing image slowly fades to black, it is with that word that we are left rather than 'The End'.

In American culture, *The King of Marvin Gardens* can be seen as a descendant of O'Neill's theater and Fitzgerald's seminal novel *The Great Gatsby* (for which role in Jack Clayton's screen adaptation Nicholson was considered before being passed over in favor of Robert Redford). But, as Jack himself might have put it, neither of these is exactly a publishing item 'to make anybody rich', and the movie enjoyed only a *succès d'estime*. It was, however, much admired in Europe — Rafelson has never been a prophet in his own country — and Ellen Burstyn received an Oscar nomination for her

Angst in Atlantic City J.N., Ellen Burstyn and Bruce Dern in The King of Marvin Gardens

The King of Marvin Gardens

performance as Sally. At the New York Film Festival, where Nicholson was spotted partaking of what Andy Warhol's *Interview* magazine quaintly described as 'raspberry snuff', the movie was greeted with enthusiasm mingled with mild perplexity.

Jack's patience and zeal were becoming legendary. When he read through a script, he would conscientiously underline key phrases, whether lines from his own dialogue or those allotted to other actors. He also liked to establish a kind of *esprit de corps* on a movie set, where his favoritism, so to speak, applied to just about everyone. 'I've never seen any other actor do it,' said Mike Nichols. 'Usually everyone has their own cliques — the camera crew, the electricians, and so on — but when Jack's around, that feeling disappears.' On occasion, Nicholson's hypertrophied sense of competition risked upsetting the general bonhomie. Rafelson recalled how, during the shooting of *The King of Marvin Gardens*, all of Nicholson's pent-up energy would be released in a marathon series of violent ping pong games with the crew. Needless to say, he demolished everyone who dared to take him on.

He began to be more selective in his choice of film, turning down those vehicles which, however attractive, might undermine his increasing determination to remain his own man. Thus, he was offered one of the leading roles in George Roy Hill's *The Sting* (eventually filmed, of course, with Paul Newman and Robert Redford), and declined it. 'I knew I could do the part well,' he explained, 'and I knew it might widen my appeal. But I don't know if I really want that at this stage. I'd still rather take different sorts of challenges than the one of becoming a bigger and bigger Jack Nicholson.'

But his position as the most glittering fish in a relatively small pond — the still somewhat marginal movies associated with BBS Productions — was perhaps beginning to frustrate him. Certainly, in these years of the early 1970s, he no longer felt much inclination to confine himself to starring roles in 'cult' films. 'We've gone through a decade of pandering to youth, letting it all fall out. But it's become a fashionable exercise and you can't do serious things and relate them to fashion. You have to be less facile than that. You owe it to an audience to be critical of them but not to exacerbate them for the sheer hell of it.'

He had been sent pre-publishing proofs of a novel by Darryl Ponicsan (whose *Cinderella Liberty* had already been filmed by Mark Rydell). It was called *The Last Detail*, and Nicholson instantly knew he wanted to play the leading role of Signalman first class 'Badass' Buddusky. Since he himself could not raise the financing for a movie version, he passed the novel on to the director Hal Ashby (who had previously been responsible for *The Landlord* with Beau Bridges and *Harold and Maude* with Bud Cort and Ruth Gordon). Ashby was an interesting choice. Though at that stage his successes, like those of Rafelson, had been of the prestige variety (*Harold and Maude*, for example, ran several years in the same tiny Left Bank cinema in Paris), and though his work had been distinguished by an abiding sympathy for marginals of every hue, Nicholson perhaps detected that Ashby was potentially a more commercial director — as he later proved, with such box-office hits as *Coming Home* and *Being There*. Ashby therefore was to be a useful bridge between Nicholson's marginal past and mainstream future.

The Last Detail's plot is a simple one. Buddusky and a black buddy, Gunner's Mate first class 'Mule' Mulhall (Otis Young), two navy 'lifers', are assigned what seems the enviable detail of escorting a dolefully naive 18-year old seaman, Larry Meadows (Randy Quaid), from their base in Norfolk, Virginia to Portsmouth Naval Prison in New Hampshire, where he is to be incarcerated for the crime of *attempting* to steal forty dollars from the polio fund (which just happened to be the pet charity of the base commander's wife). Badass and Mule anticipate whizzing their charge up north in a day or two, then devoting the rest of the week at their disposal (and their *per diem* allowances) to their own lascivious purposes. It doesn't quite work out like that, however. Through their self-assured tough-guy hides — uniforms as much as the navy blues which clothe them — the two petty officers discover that they can still be touched by the predicament in which the hapless teenager has found himself and infuriated by his lethargic resignation to it. Though the film never overtly articulates this, the cruelty of the sentence operates as an ironic reflection of their own soulless drudgery in the Navy: the word 'lifer', after all, has inescapable penal connotations. Their decision to use the whole week to initiate Meadows into the joys of alcohol (in Washington), of the big city (in New York) and of sex (in Boston) leads to a voyage of rediscovery for themselves; and, though again unstated, there is a distinct possibility that it may indeed prove to be their 'last detail'.

The outcome for Meadows of having his consciousness raised is more ambiguous, as Buddusky wryly realizes: his eight long years in the brig will be just that much harder to bear. When, during a wintry picnic in a Boston park, he makes a futile attempt to escape, his guards automatically 'revert to type', recapture him with brutal efficiency, then deliver him as ordered to the marines in Portsmouth. In this final se-quence, however, Buddusky — the Kid's fate causing him for the first time to question his own — wins one tiny but important battle. It turns out that he is more familiar with the correct

The Last Detail

bureaucratic procedures than the supercilious receiving officer. He will stay the same bad-assed Navy man, eternally one-up on his superiors, but now beginning to wonder whether *one*-up is any longer enough.

If *The Last Detail* (1974) is one of Ashby's best movies (along with that impudent squib *Being There*), it may be because it's his least soft-centered. Neither he nor scriptwriter Robert Towne lingers over the pathos of Meadows' fate or contrives to suggest that the Hemingwayes-que sentimental education offered him by Bud-dusky and Mulhall is anything other than a pro-tracted version of the last meal eaten by a con-demned man. When Meadows emerges from the brig eight years later, dishonorably discharged, he will almost certainly have been turned into an angry, frustrated criminal; and despite the crisis of self-realization which the detail provokes in Buddusky, his reasons for having signed up in the first place — his reluctance to marry and take a steady job — are still likely to hold good. Even Meadows' placid acceptance of the callously un-just sentence is treated with some subtlety. As Buddusky puts it with a shrug of his shoulders, 'Secretly, he's probably glad. On the outside too much can happen to him. All of it bad. This way the worst is over already.' No matter that the landscape through which they travel forms a cold, unfeeling, inhospitably civilian world of bleak terminals and sordid, indifferent bars, the movie is often extremely funny. The camer-aderie which develops between the three men is so vividly sketched in that Meadows' gradual release from the emotional disabilities of his kleptomania and 'sad sack' passivity is rendered wholly credible.

Much of this is due to the three central perfor-mances, with Quaid and Young so perfectly cast that Nicholson's potentially scenestealing per-formance never quite manages to unhinge the movie. He offers a brilliant characterization of a foul-mouthed, basically goodnatured loser whose choking fits of rage seldom find a satisfac-tory outlet. Ashby and Towne do grant him one wonderful moment which was obviously inspired by the diner scene in *Five Easy Pieces*. A redneck barman in Washington, determined to eject the unsavory trio, threatens to call the shore patrol — whereupon, his eyes gleaming at such a perfect opportunity, Nicholson whips out his 45, lurches over the bar and screams at him, 'I *am* the fucking shore patrol, so give this kid a drink, or I'll blow your fucking brains out!' Another small victory, maybe, but *The Last Detail* is a modest movie which never overreaches itself.

It was an enormous success, but at once ran in-to trouble on account of its dialogue, which

"...a self-assumed tough guy hides..." J.N., Otis Young and the|back of Randy Quaid's head in *The Last Detail*

realistically approximated the kind of language employed by the Navy's lower echelons. When the Navy got wind of the problem, they vetoed the cooperation routinely extended to Hollywood movie companies. Chief Justice Burger in person banned the shooting of a drunk scene on the steps of the Supreme Court. As Nicholson commented with deadpan humor, 'It isn't exactly a recruiting film.' The soundtrack was considerably bowdlerized for television screenings, with the incongruous result that Badass and Mule are reduced to venting their wrath in the mildest of 'damns!' and 'drats!' Jack also remarked, 'I was in the National Air Guard so I know about service life. I have a brother-in-law and nephews in the Navy. Whenever you play a character you draw on your own experience and the things you have been told over the years. Wherever this film has been shown, old Navy men have come up and said, "Yeah, that's how it was." ' Of Buddusky and his rage, he added, 'Oh sure, we have all met guys like that. I have had the feeling myself, but not for some years.'

The Last Detail was the American entry at the 1974 Cannes Festival, where Nicholson carried off the Best Actor Award. He was nominated for yet another Oscar, though it wasn't to happen this year either. In any case, the honor no longer particularly appealed to him — 'it makes my pulse rate mordant'. He decided that, should he be nominated again, he would not attend the ceremony — though he was not so blasé as to deny the movie buff excitement of watching the stars line up on stage. 'When Groucho Marx came on this year,' he admitted to an interviewer in 1974, 'I was genuinely moved to tears. But, knowing them as I do, I can also sympathize with George C. Scott and Brando who just didn't want to know about the whole business. To be involved means three months of sheer hell.' Even when he finally won the statuette, for his performance in Milos Forman's *One Flew Over The Cuckoo's Nest* (1975), he remained cynically detached from the tinselly hullabaloo: 'If you spend a lot of money, it is possible to get an Academy Award. I'm told that if you spend 10,000 dollars on advertising it will get you a nomination. I like the glamor of the awards as a promotional thing and I guess it is an honor as it comes from your peer group but my feelings are really tepid about the whole thing.'

Notwithstanding such carping at one of the community's most revered institutions, Jack was acquiring the habits of a Hollywood superstar, and turned up with increasing regularity in the gossip columns of two continents. Mimi Machu had long since disappeared from the scene, as had Michelle Phillips, an exquisite brunette who

(with her first husband, the singer John Phillips) had founded The Mamas and the Papas back in the Sixties and had been married for all of eight days to Dennis Hopper. Jack now entered a long-term relationship with Anjelica Huston, the daughter of director John (who was to star opposite him in Roman Polanski's *Chinatown*). They moved in together and, though their involvement with each other had to weather more than one storm, remained together for the next eight years. If Jack had never been someone who could be called 'domesticated', it is true that he no longer seemed to crave the more gregarious socializing of his early years in Hollywood. Even from his oldest friends, people with whom he had gone fifty-fifty on both triumphs and disappointments, he became increasingly remote. Anjelica phrased it neatly, 'Jack doesn't tip his hand very much.' Robert Towne (who also wrote the scenario of *Chinatown*) complained, 'We haven't had a heart-to-heart talk in a long time.' Sally Kellerman, whose friendship with Nicholson dated almost from his arrival in Hollywood, recalled how they once shared an idiotic code word which was used as a whispered greeting, 'as our private signal that we still love each other. But I haven't said "Boobs" to Jack in a couple of years.'

'The new film is a risky film; all the films I've done in the last few years have had huge risks attached to them, though fortunately people are willing to gamble on the possibility that they just might bring the big one in. The risk of this one is that the strength is in the structure of the film. There is a narrative but it's fragmented in a particular way which makes still a second or third narative point.'

Nicholson on Michelangelo Antonioni's *The Passenger* (or, in its original Italian, *Professione: Reporter*, 1975). 'The basic theme of *The Passenger* is an identity change: it deals with the area of fantasy and the subconscious in a man who says, "Why don't I just walk out of my life and become someone new tomorrow?" It deals with the releasing of all the super-psychic energy which is locked around that fantasy, and makes comments about why you can and why you can't do this, how far it's real and how far it's a fantasy. Its success depends on whether it can express a very high-flown and esoteric theme compellingly. The structure is that of a mystery; the man who chooses the change is in a very mysterious situation, and the film tries to reach out and capture an audience by shaping itself fundamentally as a very long and elaborate and elusive chase.'

Surprising as it may seem, Antonioni's later, international films may be related to those of

Hitchcock. *Blow Up* — his study of a fashionable young photographer in Swinging London who catches out of the corner of his camera lens (as one says 'out of the corner of one's eye') what might or might not have been a murder committed in a peaceful green park — can be read as a pseudo-philosophical paraphrase of Hitchcock's *Rear Window*, in which James Stewart played a photoreporter with a broken leg ('an American in plaster-of-Paris') who, idly spying on his neighbors, also seems to have caught a murderer in his sights. *Zabriskie Point*, which involved a pair of youthful fugitives (Mark Frechette and Daria Halprin) traveling across a continent torn apart by Sixties revolt, bears a remarkable resemblance to such Hitchcock chase movies as *Saboteur* and even *The Thirty-Nine Steps*.

Viewed from this angle, *The Passenger* is Antonioni's *North by Northwest*. In Hitchcock's vintage comedy-thriller, Cary Grant is forced to assume an alien identity because he hailed a hotel bellboy who happened to be paging another man. His new identity being that of a government agent, he finds himself pursued across the map of America, from Manhattan to Chicago, from the dust-choked landscapes of the Mid-West to Mount Rushmore, by both foreign spies and the State Department.

David Locke, the character played by Nicholson in *The Passenger*, actually *chooses* to turn himself in for what he imagines is a newer, brighter model. The movie begins with him at the end of his tether and closes with his (or his new identity's) death. There is a type of film whose narrative functions almost as a lengthy prologue to its final sequence. At the end of Mizoguchi's sublime masterpiece, *Sansho Dayu (Sansho the Bailiff)*, set in feudal Japan, the young hero, separated from his parents in the opening few minutes, arrives on a deserted beach where his mother, now old, haggard and blind, is mumbling pathetically to herself. As they are tearfully reunited, Mizoguchi's camera pans away — partly out of discretion, partly to frame a humble peasant cheerfully toiling at his little allotment and paying scant attention to the apparently momentous event taking place a few yards off. Another such moment can be found in Dreyer's *Ordet*, which ends with a miracle, a literal resurrection from the dead, rendered infinitely poignant by its sheer *physicality*. The penultimate, nine-minute tracking shot of *The Passenger*, one of the most extraordinary single-shot sequences in the history of the cinema, is not only the culmination but the condensation of what has preceded it. It is as if the whole film were being retold in miniature.

First things first, however. Our initial view of Locke is in a tiny desert village in Chad. He arrives alone in a Land-Rover, hoping to find his way to something or somewhere. There follows a series of gnomically inconclusive exchanges, in French, in English and even in sign language. Finding a guide — a lonely, enigmatic figure who materializes from out of the shimmering waste — Locke sets off on a five-hour hike. Then his guide disappears as soundlessly as he appeared. Locke returns to the Land-Rover, which is hopelessly lodged in the sand. Kicking the tires, pummeling the fenders, he shouts out at the isolation surrounding him, 'Shit... All right... I don't care.' This is, in a way, the film's first death — that of 'David Locke'.

Cut to a small hotel in the village. Paying a casual visit to his next-door neighbor, the dishevelled Locke discovers him dead on his ratty, tick-infested bed — probably of a heart attack. A brief flashback to an earlier conversation between these two loners reveals that Locke has come to Africa to film a television documentary on the local guerrilla war, and that the unspecified line of business in which Robertson (the dead man) was involved seemed to call for a great deal of solitary travel. Locke, startled by the physical resemblance between Robertson and himself, exchanges passports and flies back to Europe. Resurrection.

Attempting to pick up the threads of his newly adopted existence, and following the list of appointments in Robertson's diary, he journeys (as a 'passenger' in another human being's identity) to Munich, where he discovers that Robertson had been a gunrunner for an American revolutionary group; to Barcelona, where he picks up an endearingly blank French girl (Maria Schneider); through Spain with her to keep the appointments in Robertson's diary (though, strangely, no one ever turns up); and finally to Algeciras, where all these various threads are woven into a tight knot. There is also an underscripted subplot involving Locke's wife (Jenny Runacre) and her determination to track down her husband with the aid of his former TV producer (Ian Hendry).

In Algeciras, Locke/Robertson checks in at the modest Hotel de la Gloria, to be informed that his 'wife' has already arrived. Mrs Robertson, of course, is none other than Schneider. Locke explodes: 'What the hell are you doing here with me? You'd better go.' She leaves him alone, stretched out on his bed — like Robertson in that other hotel in Africa. The camera directly faces the window, which is protected by massive iron bars. Outside is a piazza, closed on its far side by a wall against which lolls an old man, idly

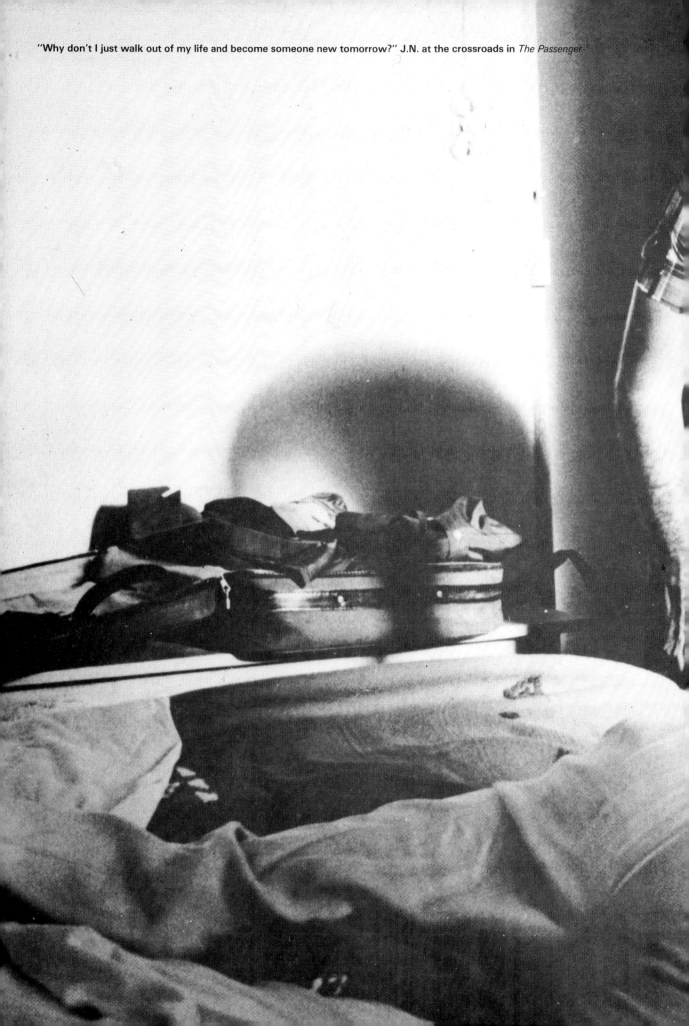

"Why don't I just walk out of my life and become someone new tomorrow?" J.N. at the crossroads in *The Passenger*

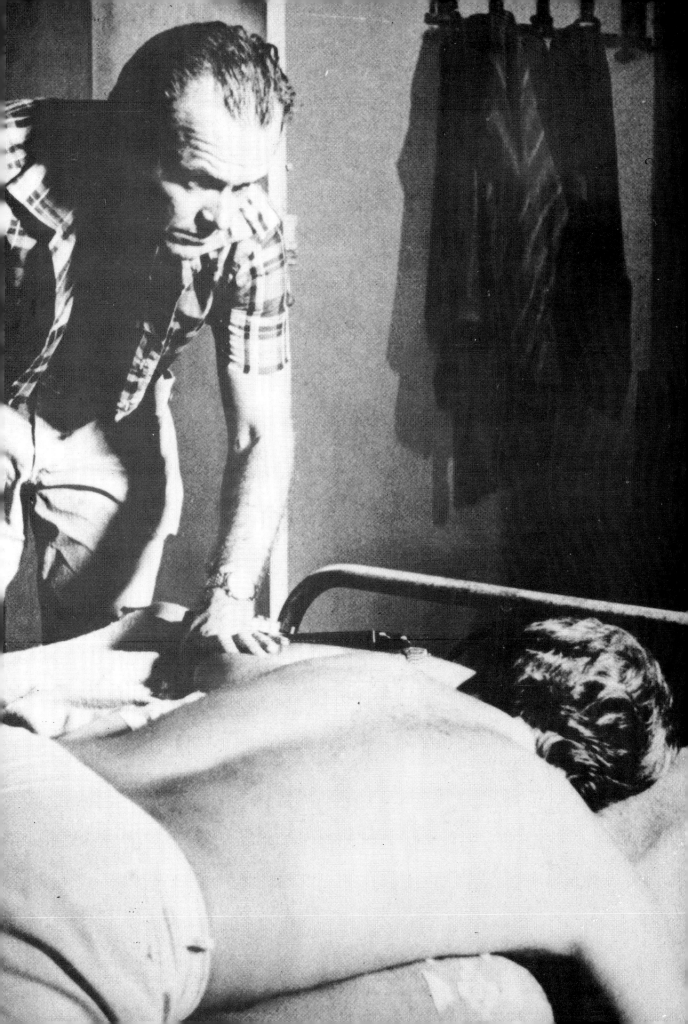

whiling away the time. Slowly, very slowly, the camera begins to advance — moving past Nicholson's supine form toward the window. We see a driving-school car unconfidently circling the square, Schneider crossing the frame, a little urchin aggressing the old man. We hear music: a pasodoble (this in a film without a real background score). The camera proceeds on its mesmeric course. Outside, a car draws up from which two men — one black, one white, both menacing — climb out. Other passers-by stop and chat to each other. The camera has almost reached the bars. Any second now, we think, Antonioni will simply have to cut. And yet, in a moment of purely filmic exaltation, the camera passes *through* the narrow space between the bars and tracks out into the square itself. Our astonishment simply at the techincial prowess required to effect such a shot is subsumed by the sense of its inevitability, of the film — like the camera movement — coming full circle. For the camera has now begun to curve back towards the hotel's entrance, panning along its facade as Locke's wife and Schneider enter together. It finally comes to a halt on reaching the wrought-iron window bars where it began: inside, Locke is still lying on the bed, now dead — presumably killed by the men trailing Robertson. With one final shot of the hotel facade at night, the film ends.

For Nicholson, involvement with a director like Antonioni proved something of a challenge. 'I found working with Antonioni a tremendous discipline. It was very hard work, and there was tension between us at times, because that's the nature of work on this kind of thing. And of course Antonioni is always very much the master. With some film-makers you feel that maybe the films have happened by some sort of accident, that perhaps critics have read into them things that aren't there. But with Antonioni what is in the films is exactly what he meant to put there. He deserves his position, and people working with him accept it — he's not holding it like a dictator, in many ways he's very open. He told me that he approaches every scene as though it were a documentary on the material of the scene; he doesn't want to leave too much of a preconception of the scene. Antonioni's basic approach to his actors is "don't act, just say the lines and make the movements". He doesn't make dramatic constructions, he makes configurations. And the simpler you can be, the clearer will be the configuration. If you mess the interior up, and so break up the interior part of your character, you will in fact be working at cross-purposes with him, because he is looking for clarity in that area, so that the configuration

"Wanna know what happens to inquisitive guys?" J.N. finds out in *Chinatown*

can be seen. If you break that up, you are working against the style in which he is working. That was hard for me to learn, but I'm glad I did it.'

Of his temperamental co-star, with whom he had a brief affair, he had this to say: 'We worked beautifully together. She used to say it was because I understood everything that was happening and she understood nothing.' Nicholson and Schneider do work together in what is for an Antonioni movie a surprisingly likable, easygoing fashion. Hers is a decidedly *un*mysterious presence, languid yet, one suspects, more resilient than is immediately apparent. They share a quiet, funny, reflective moment over two Cokes at a Spanish roadside café; the significance of the scene derives less from what is being said (though it is the first occasion on which Locke reveals his switching identities) than from its position in the movie as a rest, almost in the musical sense. For the moment, the plotline — a not always plausible salad of revolutionary politics and existential crises — is forgotten, *suspended*.

In *Chinatown*, the title turns out to be the very last word pronounced in the movie. As J. J. Gittes, a private detective in the Chandlerian, indeed Bogartian, mold, stares devastated at the gleaming white automobile in the darkened street where the woman he loves has just met with a hideous death, a friend pulls him away from the spectacle with a few haunting words: 'Forget it, Jake, it's Chinatown.' Not only because of the resigned way in which they are uttered, but coming after two and a half hours of the most densely plotted *film noir* in Hollywood history (no mean achievement!), they acquire a resonance far exceeding any purely geographical allusion. 'It's kismet,' he seems to be saying, or even 'That's life.' Though only its climax is set in Los Angeles' Chinatown district, the traditional lure of the Orient has been seeping through the whole narrative with its twin auras of romance and corruption. Like Chinatown itself, the movie is a labyrinth.

Its elegant Art Déco credits (in black-and-white) can almost be regarded as part of Polanski's *mise en scène*, as if to warn us that we are entering a world haunted by the past, both the cinema's past and that of the setting (Los Angeles in 1937). Part of *Chinatown*'s fascination lies in its hallucinatory depiction of today's sprawling mega-metropolis as, in the Thirties, fundamentally a 'small town' surrounded by rocks and arid desert. Never exploiting the past for any loving nostalgia (as witness the admirably discreet use of the period's popular music), Polanski creates a community in transition through tiny telling pinpoints of almost Surrealist detail. A sinister

scratching on the outer side of an office door proves to be the noise of a workman scraping off the name of a deceased partner; a herd of sheep are unceremoniously ushered into a startled convention hall; the roar of an express train turns out to be water gushing down a conduit pipe. Though we have seen in recent years a whole cycle of private eye reruns — *The Black Bird* with George Segal (a feeble spoof on *The Maltese Falcon*), the Harper films with Paul Newman (based on Ross MacDonald's 'Lew Archer' novels), *Farewell, My Lovely* with Robert Mitchum as a gaunt, sleepy-eyed Philip Marlowe — *Chinatown* is the only one (perhaps with Robert Altman's sarcastic commentary on the genre, *The Long Goodbye*) to have devised contemporary cinematic equivalences for the by now familiar urban disquiet of early *film noirs*.

With the opening sequences, however, we certainly appear to be on familiar ground. Lounging back in his dingy office Gittes (Nicholson) watches coolly as a harrowed client flips through some compromising snapshots of his wife. 'All right, Curly,' he says laconically as the client begins to clutch for support, 'you can't eat the Venetian blinds. I just had 'em installed Wednesday.' 'She was just no good,' moans Curly, and Gittes cheerfully agrees. Classic opening moves, sent briskly through the hoop one more time. Even more classic is the appearance of Evelyn Mulwray, a mysterious woman who hires him to shadow her errant husband. Classic, too, is the fact that she proves to be an imposter hired for purposes as yet unknown; that the real husband is duly murdered; and that the real wife (Faye Dunaway at her most icily glamorous) draws Gittes into a snarled web of intrigue ranging from civic corruption to incest by way of some bizarre encounters in a morgue, a senior citizens' home, a nocturnal waste land frequented by an evilly smirking elf (the pint-sized director himself), and an outwardly ordinary house behind whose shuttered windows we are at last permitted a glimpse of the film's horrifying secret.

En route, Gittes has been fooled into supplying evidence of meetings between Mulwray, head of Los Angeles' water and power utilities board, and an unnamed young girl. When the affair becomes a public scandal and Mulwray's body is fished from the reservoir, apparently a suicide, Gittes — already aware that the victim had recently vetoed a plan for a new dam supposedly to alleviate the city's chronic water shortage — decides to persist with the case in true private eye fashion. At the center of the whirlpool into which he is sucked is Noah Cross, Evelyn Mulwray's father *and* the father of her

J.N. as "a private detective in the Bogartian mould" in *Chinatown*

child (played with relish by John Huston), who — when asked what else, with all his wealth, he could possibly desire — jovially yet chillingly replies, 'The future.'

Though, at the movie's start, we seem to be looking over Gittes' shoulder, watching what he is watching, he soon comes to occupy the center ground through the traditional thriller device of a detective reluctantly falling in love with his client. Nicholson's dead, slot-like eyes begin to interest us more than what they are witness to; and Polanski effects a magnificent visual *coup*, a sublimely simple 'touch' yet one striking enough to make the character forever memorable. With a mocking, malevolent grin and the unwelcome question, 'Wanna know what happens to inquisitive guys?', one of Cross's henchmen (Polanski) delicately slits open Gittes' nostril. Nicholson, therefore, has to play the rest of the movie with a conspicuous white band-aid concealing his nose, a prospect that would not have appealed to most actors but which, more than any other single detail, could be said to have turned him into a superstar.

"HEEEEERE'S JOHNNY!"

Nicholson's last 1975 appearance was in a cameo role in Ken Russell's *Tommy*, based on the celebrated rock opera by Pete Townshend and The Who. Russell was considerably more at ease with rock than with genuine opera, with The Who than with Tchaikovsky *(The Music Lovers)*, Mahler *(Mahler)* and Liszt *(Lisztomania)*, the romanticism of whose music and lives he had managed to trivialize beyond recall. One of the many problems with Russell's hysterical biopics is that they seem motivated by an undisguised contempt for greatness. By portraying Tchaikovsky as a closet homosexual, Mahler as a neurotic and Liszt as no more than the Mick Jagger of his period, he not only panders to a demeaningly prurient taste for historical gossip but contrives to transform major artists into flashy media personalities on the level of . . . well, Ken Russell. To be sure, his films are made with 'style', but it's a style that even a moron can respond to. His work has the spurious urgency of texts liberally splattered with exclamation marks.

But *Tommy*, the delirious tale of a Messianic youth struck deaf, dumb and blind after witnessing the murder of his father, did not exactly lend itself to further vulgarization, and the movie constituted a genuine meeting of minds. There were the usual abominable conceits — Ann-Margret as Tommy's mother floundering in a morass of soap suds, cereal and liquid chocolate oozing

out of her television screen, Eric Clapton's grotesque faith-healing headquarters, decorated with an assortment of gratuitous Marilyn Monroe icons — but these were offset by some exhilarating set-pieces. Difficult to forget Elton John as the Pinball Wizard resplendent in a glittering outfit and gigantic lace-up boots, or Tina Turner in the Acid Queen sequence, where Tommy (vapid Roger Daltrey) is encased in a steel maiden whose every joint and orifice accommodates a drug-injecting syringe. This was material that might have been invented for Russell's feverish imagination; and, for once, one did not feel obliged to *take sides*, as in his more up-market work, either with him or with the defenseless targets of his fantasies. Nicholson played a Harley Street psychiatrist in one of the movie's quieter scenes and, all things considered, he needn't have bothered.

Tommy was perhaps in the nature of a vacation for him, and he continued to relax in *The Fortune* (1976), which was directed by Mike Nichols (of *Carnal Knowledge*) and written by Adrien Joyce (aka Carol Eastman). The trouble with 'fun movies', such as this purported to be, is that too often there seems to be more fun to be had on the set than in the cinema. Watching two top Hollywood actors (the other was Warren Beatty) having a ball is not unlike overhearing some wild party in a neighbor's apartment: ir-

J.N.'s "couch-side manner" with Ann-Margaret in *Tommy*

ritation, rather than delighted complicity, tends to be the order of the day. *The Fortune* was an attempt (contemporaneous with another turkey, Stanley Donen's *Lucky Lady*, in which Burt Reynolds, Gene Hackman and Liza Minnelli sank without trace or grace) to revive an essentially Thirties genre, the screwball comedy; but it swiftly degenerated into flat-footed farce suggesting *It Happened One Night* as played by the two least funny members of The Three Stooges.

Beatty and Nicholson were Nicky and Oscar (the latter bearing absolutely no relation to the golden statuette), a pair of inept con men who devise a plan to kidnap a runaway heiress, Frederika Quintessa Bigard, familiarly named 'Freddie' (Stockard Channing, a New York theater comedienne who represented the movie's sole asset), with the idea that Nicky would marry her and all three would live on her inheritance. Since Nicky is still waiting for his divorce papers to come through, however, it's the feeble-minded Oscar who becomes the bridegroom with Nicky posing as his brother-in-law. Friction soon develops when Oscar proves disinclined to work but more than inclined to assert his conjugal rights: and discovering that, though disinherited by her father, their scatter-brained charge is still an heiress on her mother's side, they hit on murder as the only solution to their predicament. Naturally, they bungle the job — a rattlesnake drops dead before it can poison her, she easily survives an attempt to drown her in an ornamental lily-pond — and the movie ends with the blithely unfazed heroine prepared to elope all over again.

Forty years ago, this might well have been a barrel of laughs, but the barrel had been pretty thoroughly and gratingly scraped. The knockabout brawls with which the movie was regularly punctuated soon became wearisome; the playing of the two male principals was either too broad (Nicholson in a frizzy Art Garfunkel-style hairdo for which he required a weekly permanent) or too narrow (Beatty typecast as an ambulant phallus); and Stockton Channing's closing line, on being informed by the police of her companions' murderous intentions — 'Oh no! I would never believe that in a million years!' — echoed the spectator's own sour sentiments.

To a journalist Nicholson once claimed (inaccurately, as it turned out) that he was about to take a year off. 'The last three years, out of, what, 156 working weeks, I worked 162. I was editing one project and acting in another. Anyway I was talking to Richard Burton, and I asked him how much time he'd taken off in his career. He asked, "Off off?" An actor knows what it means to take off. I said, "Yeah". He said, "Maybe six weeks."

In thirty years he's taken six weeks to himself. So I decided to take off, to watch the seasons change. You become an actor because it isn't a nine-to-five job. You expect an unscheduled existence. Then you become bankable, and you know exactly what you'll be doing four years from now. Even the President of the United States doesn't know what he'll be doing four years from now. I want to get out of that cycle for a while. Let the reservoir fill up.'

Understandable, but it wasn't to be just yet. Apart from a handful of aborted film projects — *The Border*, to be directed by Tony Richardson (eventually filmed in 1981), *Une Larme, un sourire (A Tear, a Smile)* with Jeanne Moreau, and a western which he was to direct himself, - *Moontrap*, based on a novel by Donald Barry — he almost immediately moved into the role that was finally to furnish his mantelpiece with an Oscar, that of the tragically irrepressible R. P. McMurphy in Milos Forman's adaptation of the Ken Kesey novel, *One Flew Over the Cuckoo's Nest*.

The movie had a curious genesis. Kesey's novel was published, to national acclaim, in 1962 and only one year later was dramatized for the Broadway stage with Kirk Douglas in the leading role. Douglas was eager to star in a film version himself and, while touring Eastern Europe on behalf of the State Department, he met Forman and sent him a copy of the book. It was apparently lost in transit. After a number of years trying vainly to set up the project, he turned it over to his son Michael (producer-star of *The China Syndrome*), who in turn managed to interest Saul Zaentz of Fantasy Records, a company which was just beginning to expand into film production. Douglas's intuition was right, even as to the director who could make an immense box-office success out of what was by no means an obvious commercial property.

Nicholson has played quite a few mentally unstable characters in his time, from the juvenile psychotics of his exploitation movies to the homicidal maniac of Stanley Kubrick's *The Shining* (1979), and he was reported as saying, 'I have strange fans. I get unusual confrontations in parking lots. A man comes up and says he's Tom Mix's *alter ego* and wants me to see his ghost horse. Mental illness, you know, is something different from what people think of as "crazy". When we say a man is "crazy", we think of him driving his car at 120 miles an hour through New York City. But that's quite different from somebody who is afraid to walk out the door because he fears he'll sink into the earth. Quite different from somebody who has piercing headaches, or compulsive urges to hit people, or bite

J.N. in a frizzy Art Garfunkel-style hairdo for *The Fortune* **with Warren Beatty**

them. None of these conditions is very charming or romantic. People who suffer them are separate from the rest of the world. I have been in therapy for a particular problem. Did it for a year. And making *Cuckoo* I saw every kind of mental illness.'

McMurphy, of course, is not disturbed when he enters the State Mental Hospital. Charged with assault and statutory rape — behavior he cheerfully acknowledges but just as cheerfully rationalizes — he has been transferred for observation from a penal work farm under suspicion of having simulated instability in order to avoid work detail. In the hospital, he becomes a cat among the pigeons, to the annoyance of one Nurse Ratched (Louise Fletcher), whose unceasing and tyrannical efforts to tranquillize the inmates clash with his openly declared war on their lethargy. For example, he substitutes a porno deck for the cards used in the ward; he introduces cigarettes as gambling currency; he persuades the hitherto docile patients to demand radical improvements in the strict hospital schedule; and, lastly, he organizes a truant excursion for an afternoon of deep-sea fishing from which everyone benefits hugely. It is after conflict in the ward, resulting partly from McMurphy's realization that unlike the voluntary patients he will never be free to leave, that he receives shock treatment along with Chief Bromden, a stocky, morose and apparently deaf-and-dumb Indian (Will Sampson). Bromden reveals to McMurphy, however, that his muteness is only a feint, a mechanism whereby he can withdraw from the white man's world which destroyed his father. McMurphy, determined to escape, arranges for two girls, Candy and Rose, to bring a car (laden with liquor supplies) to the hospital. There is a riotous farewell party, during which McMurphy fatally postpones his departure so that a severely repressed young inmate, Billy (Brad Dourif), might lose his virginity to Candy. The following morning sees the whole ward, to Nurse Ratched's fury, under the cloud of a massive hangover. But the situation's underlying humor rapidly turns to tragedy when Billy, surprised by the Nurse in Candy's arms, commits suicide, a now half-demented McMurphy attempts to strangle her and is left in a catatonic state after forcibly undergoing a frontal lobotomy. In an ending reminiscent of John Steinbeck's *Of Mice and Men*, the Chief, sadly contemplating the wreck of his former friend, smothers him with a pillow and prepares his own escape.

Kesey's novel forms no less a part of Sixties counterculture than the musical *Hair*, which was brought to the screen by Forman in 1979. But whereas his adaptation of the latter work was consciously conceived as a period piece, as a fuzzy memorial to an epoch already viewed through the soft focus of nostalgia, the evocation of the recent past in *Cuckoo's Nest* is strangely discreet. The movie *does* take place in the early Sixties, as evidenced by snippets of a news broadcast alluding to the Berlin Wall and race riots in Alabama, but Forman and scenarists Bo Goldman and Laurence Haubman evidently aimed to erase every trace of acid-head paranoia. This strategy has undoubted advantages. The depiction of mental instability (its authenticity reinforced by the participation as extras of staff and patients from the Oregon State Hospital, where *Cuckoo's Nest* was shot) is no longer directly equated with the unconventional behavior — hippiedom, Flower Power — of the period when the novel was written (reputedly under the influence of LSD). It cannot fail to make the spectator ponder just how applicable what he is watching remains to the treatment of the mentally ill today. And it more easily encourages audience identification with characters who are usually presented as embodiments of 'otherness', to be pitied or mocked. By the same token, however, a few of the rough edges which make the novel so nightmarishly vivid have been smoothed out. Since Kesey's vision was a subjective one, rarely submitting its insights to any realistic verification, its freaked-out, comic strip style depicted the hospital administration as a classic case of bureaucratic fascism. In a movie, especially the kind of social comedy envisaged by Forman, this would be absurd. Some kind of naturalistic base is essential.

The result is that a literary work actually *infected* by the kind of revolutionary, anti-Establishment tendencies which it both chronicles and endorses has been turned into a cinematic vehicle whereby one man takes on the System and the spectator is invited to root for him in a totally unequivocal way. Schizophrenia, the movie seems to be suggesting, can be cured with a few porno playing-cards and a deep-sea fishing expedition. A simplistic but reassuring message, which no doubt explains its extraordinary popularity. Forman himself has been quoted as saying, 'I can only define "mental illness" as an incapacity to adjust within normal measure to ever-changing, unspoken rules. If you are incapable of making these constant changes, you are called by your environment crazy.' Well, yes and no . . . But, Forman to the contrary, there *is* such a thing as mental illness (minus the quotation marks) and the assumption that it operates solely in relation to pressures from one's environment is mildly irresponsible

J.N. with 'Scatman' Crothers in *One Flew Over the Cuckoo's Nest*

— to put it mildly.

No complaints, though, about Nicholson's Oscar-winning, Oscar-deserving performance. From our first glimpse of him shattering the hygienic, white-walled silence of the hospital with a strident burst of laughter and planting a kiss on the astonished features of the accompanying warder to the virtuoso sequence where he offers a group of cheering patients a baseball commentary in front of a blank TV screen which, dimly reflecting its excited audience, seems to come alive even for the spectator, he so completely invested himself in McMurphy that it became impossible to imagine any other actor playing the role. In fact, he made such a convincing show of undergoing shock treatment that a complaint was registered by a senior medical officer concerning what he believed was cruelty to the actors. But as Michael Douglas, the film's producer, drily remarked, 'After eight weeks filming at the hospital you could not tell the actors from the inmates, unless you had a program.'

One Flew Over the Cuckoo's Nest won six Golden Globe Awards and an Oscar for Jack (whose principal competitor was apparently Al Pacino as the homosexual bank robber of Sidney Lumet's *Dog Day Afternoon*). Talking to an English journalist just prior to the ceremony,

Nicholson did not rate his chances too highly. 'The people who vote for these things don't like me much. You see, I don't spend my time doing charity work. And that's very important to the Academy. The *image* you create. It's not that I've anything against charitable work. It's just that I don't have the time. And, of course, they also think I'm a bit of a rebel. Which I guess is true. Mind you, I'm not the rebel I used to be. I'm 39 years old. I do have a suit I wear occasionally.' Their conversation was interrupted by a telephone call which he took in his bedroom. Returning, he explained, 'That was a call from a girl named Suzy whom I have never met in my life before. She said she's a friend of a friend and what was I doing this evening because she was feeling a bit bored. I told her she'd got on to the wrong guy.'

Nicholson's private life was again receiving wide public coverage. Anjelica had left him *twice* for the actor Ryan O'Neal, managing to pass the acid test of being approved by his formidable daughter Tatum. 'I was upset about it at the time,' he said, 'but I'm not now. When you have a problem like that you can only deal with it and move on.' Oddly enough, both her abrupt departures appear to have been provoked by his proposing marriage. More sensational was the arrest, the following year, of Roman Polanski on the charge of raping a 13-year-old girl in Nicholson's house. Jack himself was absent at the time (he had recently purchased another house in Colorado) but Anjelica, back in residence, was also arrested for possession of cocaine. Besides the question of rape, Polanski was booked on charges of sodomy, child molestation and furnishing dangerous drugs to a minor. Having been taken into custody at the Beverly Wiltshire Hotel in Beverly Hills, where he was staying, he was released on the surprisingly modest bail of 2,500 dollars. In return for testifying against him, Anjelica was subsequently cleared of any involvement in the case; but Polanski, after being placed under observation in a hospital, succeeded in slipping out of the United States. Though he promised from time to time that he would eventually return and stand trial, he has never set foot on American soil to this day (except for a single embarrassing occasion when he spent a few hours in Los Angeles airport without his presence being detected by the authorities). Jack defended his friend thus: 'He has already spent more time inside than other people who have admitted to the same offence. He is paying for the fact that he is a name.' Which is a refreshingly original way of looking at it...

Nicholson followed *One Flew Over The Cuckoo's Nest* with a strange movie, Arthur Penn's *The Missouri Breaks* (1976), in which he co-starred with his next-door-neighbor and long-term idol, Marlon Brando. Rumor has it that both were offered over a million dollars for just ten weeks work, causing Jack to sigh philosophically at the end of each working day, 'Another day, another 20,000 dollars...' (Upon completion of filming, however, he sued the producer, Elliott Kastner, over the little matter of a further million dollars which he claimed was owed him.)

The Missouri Breaks, written by the novelist Thomas McGuane, offered a choice example of that curious and rarely satisfying hybrid, the comic Western. Its somewhat quirky brand of humor was established early on when a wealthy rancher returns home following a lynching session and, settling down in his plush library of classics, casually turns to his daughter: 'Pull down *Tristram Shandy* again for me, would you?' In a later sequence, a second rustler about to be hanged wistfully remarks that, after his death, he'd like to be known as 'The Lonesome Kid'. Though the basic plot of *The Missouri Breaks* was in no way unconventional, its clownish tone permitted the characters, quite as much as Penn and McGuane, to maintain an ironic distance from all the hallowed myths of the American West even as they were forging them.

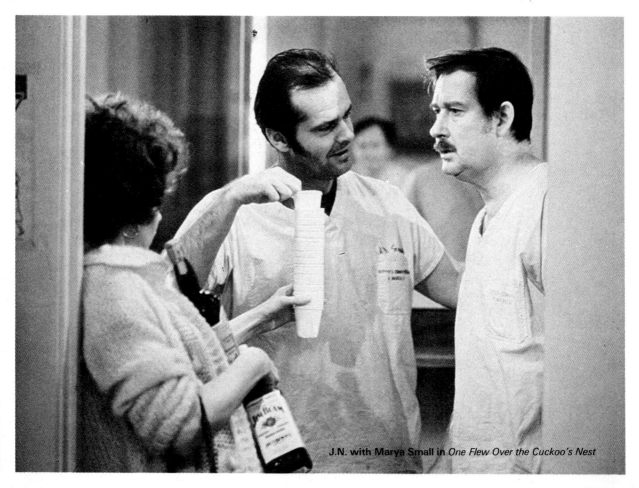

J.N. with Marya Small in *One Flew Over the Cuckoo's Nest*

J.N. with director Arthur Penn on the set of *The Missouri Breaks*

J.N. with Marlon Brando "in outrageous granny drag" in *The Missouri Breaks*

This applies above all to Brando as Robert E. Lee Clayton, the rancher's sadistic 'Regulator'. Brando is on record as having found in his character the 'opportunity for a serious study of the American Indian', but it isn't easy to see where his preposterous creation — a perfumed, Irish-accented Buffalo Bill who is not averse to stalking his prey in outrageous granny drag — could be inserted into the history of the Indian massacres. Though critics are fond — maybe over-fond — of the word 'self-indulgent' to describe any writer, director or actor who refuses to bend to the prevailing mediocrity, the word is entirely apposite here. To judge his performance in the codified terms of 'goodness' or 'badness' would be irrelevant. It's both and neither; and if 1,500,000 dollars could be considered a rather steep fee for giving an actor the chance to let his hair down, the spectator at least got value for his money at the box-office. (Since *The Missouri Breaks* was a flop, the moviegoing public obviously decided otherwise.)

Brando was, as they say, *something else*: bird-watching atop his horse with a pair of field-glasses in one hand, an illustrated manual in the other; interrupting a funeral to filch the ice in which the deceased has been packed in order to apply it to an aching tooth; taunting a charred rustler whom he has just incinerated in his cabin with the single, unanswerable insult, 'Smoke-meat!' Most memorable is his death scene, when he suddenly wakes up to find Nicholson whispering silkily in his ear, 'You know what woke you up? Well, you've just had your throat cut.' Beside Brando's unrelenting barrage of campy behavioral tics, Nicholson — as the ringleader of a gang of rustlers — found himself relegated more or less to the role of stooge, one that he performed with such good grace in his lazily drawling manner that he succeeded in rustling back a few scenes from his scenestealing partner. It was a minor performance in what could only be described as a minor Western, but it was good to feel that the talent remained intact.

He played another supporting role in Elia Kazan's star-studded adaptation of F. Scott Fitzgerald's uncompleted novel, *The Last Tycoon* (also 1976). Harold Pinter's literate if slightly stilted script (writers, no less than actors, can be miscast) brought its narrative to a close at the point where Fitzgerald's manuscript fell silent, without making use of the numerous suggestions left behind in rough draft. Such discretion was symptomatic of the movie's too literal, awe-struck approach to the novel, whose indefinable, gauzy charm would seem in any case to be resistant to cinematic transcription. Pinter's dialogue sounded incongruously like some of Fitzgerald's own unhappy excursions into screenwriting, and the amusing scene in which his Wunderkind hero Monroe Stahr (based on MGM's celebrated 'genius in residence' of the Thirties, Irving Thalberg, and smoothly played by Robert De Niro) chides an imported British novelist (Donald Pleasance) for having written pedantically 'unspeakable' dialogue had rather a hollow ring in a film which suffered from the same problem. The interpolated movie-within-a-movie sequences — excerpts from some sudsy romantic melodrama with Jeanne Moreau and Tony Curtis — were invested with a vague 'sense of period' which Kazan chose never to pin down; while *The Last Tycoon*'s own romantic interludes — when Stahr, for example, invites the virginal Kathleen (Ingrid Boulting) to his half-completed seashore retreat and she runs barefoot in the grass — might have registered more strongly if they had possessed just a hint of frank TV commercial vulgarity.

Nicholson played the marginal role of a studio union organizer, and his larger-than-life presence was welcome in a movie that seemed to be embalming its prestigious but problematic source material rather than kissing (or kicking) it back into existence.

In 1978, Jack was ready to direct again, and this time he prepared to direct himself. The property he selected, *Goin' South*, was an irreverent little romantic comedy set among the Dakota Badlands in the late nineteenth century. With outer space an increasingly familiar landscape on the screen and Michael Cimino's *Heaven's Gate* about to bite the dust as the most spectacular flop in a period of Hollywood's history littered with spectacular flops, a Western was a courageous undertaking. Nicholson, however, knew what he wanted and why he wanted it. 'The cowboy hero symbolizes the single, unchallenged fact of the universe,' he declared rather grandly, 'the loneliness of every single man. Everything else in life is designed to cover up that fact. This is a little human story I knew I could make, and I knew I could act in. For my character I used everyone from Gabby Hayes to Spencer Tracy. Tracy is my favorite comic.' And he added with some justification, 'What is stardom for if you don't take chances?'

Goin' South starts where many a Western has ended: with a lynching. As it happens, though, its 'hero', Henry Lloyd Moon — fifth-rate outlaw, ex-cook and dishwasher with Quantrill's Raiders and unsuccessful applicant to the Younger Gang — is rescued from the noose when he is chosen as her mate by an unattached lady of property, Julia (Mary Steenburgen): it seems so many menfolk had perished in the Civil War that

J.N.'s "larger than life presence" in *The Last Tycoon*

J.N. rescued from the gallows in *Goin' South*

the law offered this quaint solution to lonely, willing (and foolhardy) spinsters. After what is literally a shotgun wedding, we follow the droll misadventures of this ill-matched pair at odds with pursuing lawmen, Moon's former cronies — and each other. Moon, offended at being set to work on Julia's mine as if he were not her husband at all but an unpaid employee, attempts to charm his way into her virginal bed. In the event, as a curious mirror image of the opening scene, he is obliged to attach her to that bed with another piece of rope before making love to her. As is proper in a comedy, however, all ends happily with Moon and Julia reunited and, as the title predicted, 'goin' south' across the border to Mexico.

Though influenced by Nicholson's stint on *The Missouri Breaks* (as well as by the ecological romanticism of *Easy Rider* and *Five Easy Pieces*), *Goin' South* fuses the mythic elements of the American cinema's most authentic genre with post-Sixties anarchy far more likably than Penn's film. Here the humor derives from the conflict of character and situation rather than from the intervention of a farcically surreal individual such as Brando played. 'It is difficult directing yourself in comedy,' Nicholson told journalist Glenys Roberts, who visited the set in Durango, 'because you have no idea whether you are going over the top. That last scene I played entirely with my head in a black bag. It was difficult enough keeping on the mark.' When the actor-director inquired of those around him how the scene had gone, Roberts reported that he was greeted by a chorus of 'Terrifics' and suggested that, with so much spare, yes-man enthusiasm lying around, a good deal of the footage couldn't help but 'go over the top'. But he added that, in view of the excessive number of takes for each shot (one three-word interjection by Steenburgen required no fewer than sixteen before Jack was happy), the tyro was assuming his double role with justified caginess. Anything that proved to be unworkable would bite the dust on the cutting-room floor, and the contrasting moods by which the movie is cohabited mesh together gracefully.

All of these moods were encapsulated in Nicholson's brilliant performance. He could be both funny and touching, lyrical and fantastic, treating us in one scene to a virtuoso display of eye-rolling and face-pulling that climaxes in his frantic endeavors to convince his wife that he is not at all enjoying himself while cutting some manic capers to entertain his old gang. Were it not for his impressive catalog of past achievements in drama, one would have been tempted to believe that he had missed his voca-

tion as a primarily *comic* performer. *Goin' South* demonstrates conclusively that Jack Nicholson is a very funny man.

The movie busted no blocks, as it were, at the box-office. But, given the assurance with which it was directed, Jack was in an unduly pessimistic mood when he commented, 'If this film doesn't work I can never direct again. *Drive, He Said* was not a commercial success. You can never blame the audience. A good film always finds its audience. This movie is tiring me. I don't think I'll ever make another.'

Tired or not, Nicholson dashed from one film to another as if his life depended on it. Producers David Brown and Richard Zanuck announced that he was on their shortlist (in company with Burt Reynolds and Sean Connery) to play Rhett Butler in a proposed remake of *Gone With The Wind*. He had now become, as he only half-jokingly defined himself, a '*mega*-superstar', whose every antic seemed of urgent concern to the international press. (On one occasion, when he suddenly rose from his table at Sardi's, he was tailed by a veritable posse of *paparazzi* screaming, 'Where's he going? Where's he going?' Jack halted for a moment; then, with admirable aplomb, replied in a tone that was audible to the whole restaurant, 'To the bathroom.' The 'incident' was widely reported.) When he was required in London for shooting on his next movie, Stanley Kubrick's *The Shining*, the production company, Hawk Films, rented a luxuriously appointed house for him in Cheyne Walk at a cost of 850 pounds (or almost 2,000 dollars) a week. Situated on the Chelsea Embankment, it boasted four bedrooms, four bathrooms, four reception rooms and a lush garden which, with its sliding roof, could double as a dining room. It was during his sojourn there that he rashly attempted to scale a low garden wall, suffered a heavy fall and caused a few days of consternation to Kubrick and his backers.

Kubrick had first been intrigued by the up-and-coming actor as early as his first appearance in *Easy Rider*. He was then planning a film biography of Napoleon (a project which was eventually diverted into his adaptation of Thackeray's *Barry Lyndon*) and one fine morning rang up a sleepy Nicholson. 'This is Stanley Kubrick,' he solemnly presented himself. 'I just saw *Easy Rider*. Now I'm working on *Napoleon*, and my assumption is that the prejudice of American audiences is that they only want to see actors in classical stories with English accents. But now I've had ten days to think about your performance and you have one quality which can't be *acted* as an actor. You cannot create intelligence within a characterization for an actor.

J.N.'s ''smarmy interview'' with Barry Nelson and Philip Stone in *The Shining*

J.N. as a ''grand guignol ogre'' with Shelley Duvall in *The Shining*

You *have* it tremendously, it's obvious, it permeates your work.'

Which remark, though sagacious, was a curious one for Kubrick to make. If the role he finally offered Nicholson, that of an alcoholic novelist *manqué* who accepts the post of caretaker for the winter in the massive, labyrinthine Overlook Hotel high in the Colorado Mountains, possessed various qualities, intelligence was not conspicuous among them. *The Shining*, based on Stephen King's bestselling horror novel, describes how Jack Torrance, isolated with his wife (Shelley Duvall) and young son (Danny Lloyd), begins to establish contact of a kind with the grisly spirits who haunt the hotel's vacant rooms and endless, echoing corridors. An empty lounge is mysteriously populated by a crowd of Jazz Age revelers presided over by a leering barman; the child is 'befriended' by the murdered twin daughters of the previous caretaker who was apparently driven berserk by the snowbound isolation; and Torrance himself, straying into the dreaded room 237, is embraced by a beautiful young woman who is suddenly transformed into a decaying corpse. Half-crazed by his inability to write (on glancing at his manuscript, his wife discovers that it contains only the phrase 'All work and no play makes Jack a dull boy' repeated *ad nauseam*), the axe-wielding Torrance begins to terrorize his petrified family. In the movie's penultimate image, he is revealed frozen stiff in the ornamental maze just outside the hotel. Its final shot consists of a slow zoom into a framed photograph of the Overlook in its Twenties heyday: located dead center is none other than Jack Torrance.

Though in some respects an interesting, even an absorbing work, *The Shining* is far from unflawed. Especially as he usually withdraws into two or three years of heavily-guarded seclusion to make a movie, Kubrick was guilty of a tactical blunder in announcing that his special effects would be the most terrifying in cinema history. They weren't. By the movie's release date, the horror vogue had long since overtaken that ambition with visceral assaults on audience sensibilities of unparalleled sadism (eg *Alien*). Kubrick's effects turned out to be a derivative, none too frightening joblot of stale haunted house leftovers.

He made other major miscalculations: his decision to use such composers as Bartok, Ligeti and Penderecki on the soundtrack suggested some spurious (and philistine) parallel between primal horror and the discords of contemporary music; despite being highlighted by the title, the little boy's extrasensory gift of 'the shining' plays only a peripheral role in the narrative; and the dénouement, as banal as it is enigmatic, neither satisfies the spectator with a logical solution nor encourages him to rethink his interpretation of what preceded it. In counterbalance was the magnificent deployment of an equally magnificent set, with Kubrick sending his flexible Steadicam apparatus along the corridors in a breathtaking whizz; or, in the movie's single most striking scene (worthy of the celebrated bone-to-spaceship cut in *2001*), cutting from wife and child exploring the real maze to Torrance staring down at a table-top model of it while two tiny figures appear to animate its diminutive topography. And there was Nicholson's own performance. Though criticized yet again for going over the top in the first half-hour and staying perched up there throughout the rest of the running time, it can be instructively compared to that of Shelley Duvall as his frail, highly-strung wife. Duvall, an excellent actress in Robert Altman's films, screams and rants so grotesquely as to make Fay Wray (King Kong's victim) seem a model of genteel tact. The magazine *Film Comment* sarcastically remarked that in 1980 she had played both of the Oyl sisters: Olive in Altman's *Popeye* and Garg in *The Shining*.

But Nicholson succeeds in investing his *grand guignol* ogre with an astonishing variety of inflections, from his initial smarmy interview with the hotel proprietors to the genuinely unsettling moment when he squeezes his slack, rubbery features through a battered-in door and screeches, '*Heeeeere's* Johnny!' He once confessed to having been influenced less by the character as written by Stephen King than by the old EC comics, gory rags clandestinely devoured by adolescents behind school textbooks or under bedcovers, and he perfectly catches the heartstopping quality — halfway between a *frisson* and a giggle — of all effective representations of terror. So that he might have the desired appearance of disheveled lunacy, Kubrick ordered him to stay out of the sun. He soon acquired an unhealthy pallor and remained brutishly unshaven for weeks on end.

Asked by Roderick Mann about the movie's reviews Nicholson admitted: 'Well, you know, I'm extremely thin-skinned about most of the things I read about myself. All I have to do is read a review which starts "The predictable Nicholson" and I want to quit. I want to say: that's it.' But though *The Shining* wasn't the success it ought to have been (that is, the success Hollywood expected it to be), it had a very creditable career, with Jack even claiming it as his most profitable movie since *One Flew Over the Cuckoo's Nest*.

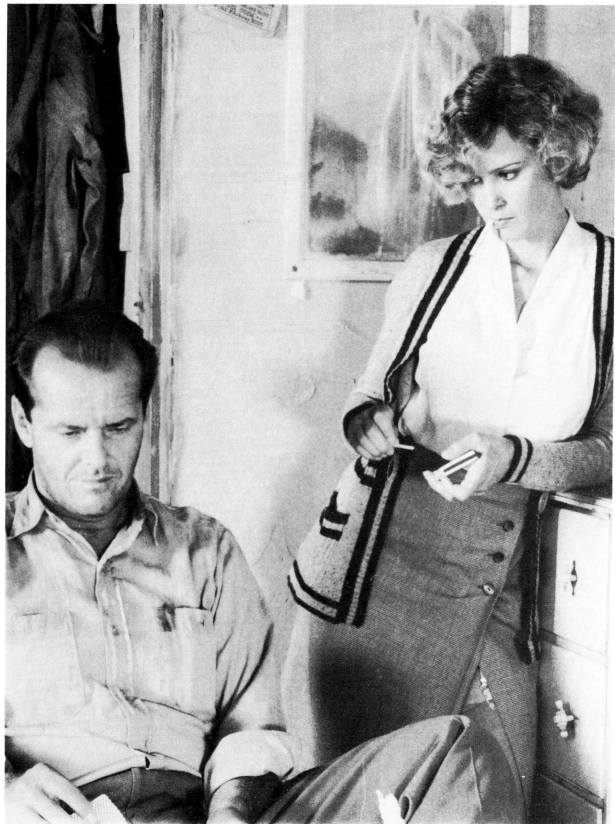

J.N.'s "aimless drifter" with Jessica Lange in *The Postman Always Rings Twice*

How he managed it is anybody's guess but, during the following year — besides being photographed in the company of Anjelica, a Marilyn Monroe lookalike named Linda Kerridge, Rachel Ward (the Earl of Dudley's niece), Princess Caroline of Monaco and singer Petula Clark's 17-year-old daughter Cathy, besides turning up in Margaret Trudeau's kiss-and-tell autobiography and being linked in gossip columns with Princess Margaret — he became involved at the start of the Eighties with two new films, Warren Beatty's *Reds* and Bob Rafelson's *The Postman Always Rings Twice*.

Since *Reds* soared over budget *and* over its

planned shooting schedule, it was Rafelson's thriller which was the first to be released. James M. Cain's steamy novel of lust and murder in Southern California during the Depression had already been filmed three times, in France, as *Le Tournant* (directed by the journeyman Pierre Chenal), in Italy as Luchino Visconti's masterly *Ossessione* (a work often credited with having launched the neo-realist movement), and in Hollywood with John Garfield and Lana Turner under the direction of Tay Garnett. That first American adaptation has been judged both a masterpiece and a travesty, perhaps because its remarkable fidelity to the original was smudged in two crucial areas: Lana Turner, a bizarrely shimmering apparition in the drably realistic settings, looked as if she had wandered onto the wrong sound stage; and the theme of sexual passion, the essential motivation for the couple's descent into criminality, suffered immeasurably from the Hays Code's repressive guidelines. For the role of the sluttishly beautiful Cora, Rafelson chose Jessica Lange, hitherto best known for having aroused King Kong's ardor in Dino de Laurentis' ill-fated remake. Another early contender was Meryl Streep who, questioned by Jack on her readiness to appear nude for the now notorious tussle on a kitchen table, coolly replied, 'I don't mind as long as you're nude too.' But Nicholson was delighted with Lange. 'She's got that terrific farm-girl-goes-to-the-city aura,' he told Roderick Mann. 'She is solid and substantial with a kind of rolling femaleness.' Lange did reveal a tawdry, dank sexuality totally opposed to the remote platinum bitch-goddess personified by Lana Turner. If her frenzied lovemaking in the kitchen carried a slightly stilted lets-show-them-what-she-really-did-now-that-there's-no-more-censorship feel to it, the carnality was authentic enough.

As the lean, aimless drifter trapped in a situation which spirals out of his control, Nicholson seemed almost a facsimile of Garfield in the earlier movie: that's to say, his performance was very good but a shade *déjà vu*. Though he had often demonstrated that he could be the most sheerly *contemporary* actor of his generation (in *Five Easy Pieces, The King of Marvin Gardens* and *The Passenger*), here as in *Chinatown* his voice, his gestures, his very facial features took on an uncanny Thirties style. As for the film, it was tolerably gripping (given a plot by now as familiar as that of *Camille*), evocatively photographed by Sven Nykvist and very well scripted by the dramatist David Mamet — and when it was all over, one felt rather like asking for one's money back. Maybe the postman had rung once too often.

Nicholson capped it, however, with one of his most memorable characterizations, as the cynical, funny, boozing, lecherous Eugene O'Neill in Warren Beatty's lengthy biopic of America's most celebrated card-carrying Communist (and author of *Ten Days That Shook the World*), John Reed. It was titled, with almost parodic terseness, *Reds*. For Beatty, whose sole previous directorial credit (with Buck Henry) had been the abysmal comic fantasy *Heaven Can Wait*, to have tackled such an ambitious

J.N. as a ''facsimile of John Garfield'' in *The Postman Always Rings Twice*

subject at all immediately put one on his side. And with the movie's budget topping the thirty million dollar mark there was little sense in reproaching him, in his depiction of the momentous events which overtook Russia *circa* 1917, for having preferred the romantic sweep of Lean's *Doctor Zhivago* to the dialectical *montage* of Eisenstein's *October*. Those critics who grumbled that the Russian Revolution sequences were rather *less* spectacular than might have been expected, that the mammoth budget simply 'wasn't there up on the screen', would doubtless have accused Beatty of having sold out to mindless Hollywood razzmatazz if he had been prepared to gratify them with grandiose imagery. What *Reds* attempted — the fusion of an unwieldy drama of ideas with an intensely felt love story, neither element being foregrounded at the other's expense — was extremely difficult, and if Beatty didn't quite bring it off, what he did achieve was worth three-and-a-half hours of anybody's time.

"...descent into criminality..." J.N. with Jessica Lange in *The Postman Always Rings Twice*

Courageously, the movie even risked alienating an unmotivated spectator from the very beginning. As a haunting Scott Joplin rag fades out over the opening credits, voices fade in, contemporary voices attempting confusedly to pin down the past. These belong to the movie's Witnesses, who form a stereophonic Greek chorus emerging from time to time during the narrative to situate the film in a historical perspective. Though they are unnamed (an error, this), one should have no problem in recognizing Rebecca West, George Jessel in his USO uniform, the mandarin sensuality of the late Henry Miller, the leathery good humor of columnist Adela Rogers St John. Thereafter, Beatty and his co-scenarist, the English dramatist Trevor Griffiths, whisk us from the chintzy parlors and genteel drawing rooms of Reed's upper-middle-class origins in Portland to a Bohemian Greenwich Village of intellectual salons and coffee-house anarchy, from Eugene O'Neill and Susan Glaspell in Provincetown to the blood-dyed quicksands of Europe's World War I battlefields — then finally to the revolutionary ferment of Petrograd in 1917. En route, we encounter along with Reed such notables of the period as Max Eastman, the crusading editor of *The Masses* (Edward Herrmann), the pugnacious radical feminist Emma Goldman (Maureen Stapleton), Zinoviev, the cynically cunning chief of the Soviet Comintern (brilliantly played by the novelist Jerzy Kosinski), and the journalist Louise Bryant (Diane Keaton), with whom Reed falls in love. It is a tribute to these performers that they impress us as scarcely less 'authentic' than the 32 Witnesses whose interventions punctuate their fictional scenes together. Keaton, who has to shake off inapposite echoes of Woody Allen's Manhattanite neuroses and, even more uncomfortably of his *Love and Death*, perhaps fails to take the measure of her role until the moment when Bryant, realizing that Reed's commitment to the advancing socialist movement will always take precedent over their on-again-off-again relationship, seeks solace with O'Neill. From that point, her playing is charged with (for this actress) an unaccustomed eroticism that allows her reconciliation with Reed, after he has delivered a rousing speech to a crowd of Bolsheviks, to triumph over considerable odds (not the least of which are the strains of the 'Internationale' wafting up from the square below). Beatty's performance, too, matures with the deepening of their relationship in the second half, where he manages to rid himself of the charmingly sexy boyishness with which he begins the movie, and which bears little resemblance to contemporary accounts of Reed.

But its best, most plausible impersonation is without question that of Nicholson as the caustic O'Neill: as Peter Rainer wrote in the *Los Angeles Herald Examiner*, 'he has such impacted carnal force that he practically burns a hole in the screen'. The hard sensuality of his exchanges with Keaton (a reflection of an affair taking place offscreen) suggest that they might, if they wanted to, become the Tracy and Hepburn of the Eighties. His taunting sarcasm toward Reed's idealism, as he plays devil's advocate to the younger man's aspirations, is wickedly, almost sadistically, funny (and benefits from the fact that Beatty and Griffiths assigned him the most trenchant dialogue in a script that does not always avoid the platitudinous or explicative). O'Neill is only a cameo, perhaps, but an actor's dream: one keeps hoping wistfully during the film that he might somehow pop up in revolutionary Russia.

As director, Beatty makes mistakes, bad ones. There are far too many obsequiously cuddly visual motifs: bouquets of white lilies, taxis in the snow, tearful partings on packed railway platforms, and one overpoweringly cute child; a howler of a cut from the distraught Reed (who has just been abandoned by Bryant) to, of all unlikely things, a puppy dog; and an occasional glut of ill-digested (and indigestible) theorizing in the dialogue. But with a soundtrack score by Stephen Sondheim, Vittorio Storaro's smoky photography and sparky walk-ons from such as George Plimpton and Gene Hackman, who's counting?

Released only a couple of months after Beatty's splashy epic, *The Border* proved to be a relatively modest tale of a tired ex-Forest Service officer (Nicholson) persuaded by his middle-aged Barbie doll of a wife to join the more lucrative Border Patrol in Texas. His job ostensibly consists of rounding up truckloads of Mexican peasants desperately in search of any kind of living on the greener side of the frontier; but he soon learns with disgust that most of his colleagues are in cahoots with the agricultural businessmen who hire wetbacks at numbingly low wages and that a patrolman's primary duty is to look the other way. The expected personal revolt — this is a Jack Nicholson movie, after all — is triggered off by a heart-stoppingly beautiful young Madonna (Elpidia Carrillo), who might have stepped out of a painting by Murrillo but is in reality wretchedly quartered with her baby in an encampment on the wrong side of the Rio Grande. In a near-suicidal mission to recover her stolen child, he finds himself taking on both his closest buddy (Harvey Keitel) and his bloated, corrupt

J.N. with Diane Keaton in *Reds*

superior (Warren Oates). His crusade is not sexually motivated: as he puts it, "I guess I gotta feel good about something I do."

Though the movie, directed with surprising conviction by the English expatriate Tony Richardson from a screenplay by Deric Washburn, Walon Green and David Freeman, generates a lot of the anger of those old Warner Bros. social melodramas in the 30s, it manages to keep its temper throughout, thereby making its indictment all the more effective. The same cool reticence informs the lively, occasionally acerbic characterizations, from Perrine with her bogus aspirations toward poolside high life to Carrillo who manages to convey naturalness without cloying cuteness. Nicholson himself, making up for thinning hair with a tight, very un-Zapata moustache, could easily have coasted along on the accumulated resonance of past performances — notably his not too dissimilar one in

The Last Detail. But he makes his quixotic volte-face as convincing as the minor-league, only half-reluctant grubbiness that precedes it, and as Richard Corliss wrote in *Time*, "he shows again that he can embody as much of the twentieth century American male — sexy, psychotic, desperate, heroic — as any movie star today".

Jack Nicholson has also been a taker of risks, and for the health of the American cinema and the sanity of its public, one can only hope that he will long continue to do so. But perhaps we need not worry too much about his periodic bouts of pessimism, as when he remarked to Glenys Roberts on the set of *Goin' South* that he didn't think he'd ever make another movie. By the following morning, with the crew ready to snap into action, their tequila hangovers cured with a breakfast of unfried eggs, Jack broke into a playful grin: 'What? Never make another movie? That was last night!'

FILMOGRAPHY

1958

CRY BABY KILLER
Allied Artists USA
Director: Jus Addiss **Producer:** David Kramarsky, David March **Screenplay:** Leo Gordon, Melvin Levy (Based on a story by Leo Gordon) **Photography:** Floyd Crosby **Editor:** Irene Morra **Music:** Gerald Fried **Song:** Dick Kallman **Cast:** Harry Lauter (Porter) Jack Nicholson (Jimmy) Carolyn Mitchell (Carole) Brett Halsey (Manny) Lynn Cartwright (Julie) Ralph Reed (Joey) John Shay (Gannon)

1960

LITTLE SHOP OF HORRORS
Santa Clara USA
Director: Roger Corman **Producer** Roger Corman **Screenplay:** Charles. B. Griffith **Photography:** Arch Dalzell **Editor:** Marshall Neilan Jnr **Music:** Fred Katz **Cast:** Jonathan Haze (Seymour Krelboind) Jackie Joseph (Audrey) Mel Welles (Gravis Mushnick) Dick Miller (Fouch) Myrtle Vail (Winifred) Leola Wendorff (Mrs Shiva) Jack Nicholson (Wilbur Force)

TOO SOON TO LOVE
Dynasty Films USA
Director: Richard Rush **Producer:** Mark Lipsky **Screenplay:** Lazlo Gorog, Richard Rush **Photography:** William Thompson **Editor:** Stephen Arnsten **Music:** Ronald Stein **Cast:** Jennifer West (Cathy Taylor) Richard Evans (Jim Mills) Warren Parker (Mr Taylor) Ralph Manza (Hughie Winemann) Jack Nicholson (Buddy) Jacqueline Schwab (Irene)

STUDS LONIGAN
Longridge Enterprises USA
Director: Irving Lerner **Producer:** Philip Yordan **Screenplay:** Philip Yordan (Based on the STUDS LONIGAN Trilogy by James T. Farrell) **Photography:** Arthur Feindel **Editor:** Verna Fields **Music:** Gerrald Goldsmith **Cast:** Christopher Knight (Studs Lonigan) Frank Gorshin (Kenny Killarney) Venetia Stevenson (Lucy Scanlon) Carolyn Craig (Catherine Banahan) Jack Nicholson (Weary Reilly) Robert Casper (Paulie Haggerty) Dick Foran (Patrick Lonigan)

THE WILD RIDE
Filmgroup USA
Director: Harvey Berman **Producer:** Harvey Berman **Screenplay:** Ann Porter, Marion Rothman **Photography:** Taylor Sloan **Editor:** William Mayer **Cast:** Jack Nicholson (Johnny Varron) Georgianna Carter (Nancy) Robert Bean (Dave)

1962

THE BROKEN LAND
Associated Producers USA
Director: John Bushelman **Producer:** Leonard Schwartz **Screenplay:** Edward Lakso **Photography:** Floyd Crosby **Editor:** Carl Pierson **Music:** Richard LaSalle **Cast:** Kent Taylor (Jim Kogan) Dianna Darrin (Mavra Aikens) Jody McCrea (Ed Flynn) Robert Sampson (Gabe Dunson) Jack Nicholson (Will Broicous) Gary Snead (Billy Bell)

1963

THE RAVEN
Alta Vista / American International USA
Director: Roger Corman **Producer:** Roger Corman **Screenplay:** Richard Matheson (Based on the poem by Edgar Allan Poe) **Photography:** Floyd Crosby **Editor:** Ronald Sinclair **Music:** Les Baxter **Cast:** Vincent Price (Dr Erasmus Craven) Peter Lorre (Dr Bedlo) Boris Karloff (Dr Scarabus) Hazel Court (Lenore Craven) Olive Sturgess (Estelle Craven) Jack Nicholson (Roxford Bedlo) Connie Wallace (Maid Servant)

THE TERROR
Grand National Pictures USA
Director: Roger Corman **Producer:** Roger Corman **Screenplay:** Leo Gordon, Jack Hill **Photography:** John Nickolaus **Editor:** Stuart O'Brien **Music:** Ronald Stein **Cast:** Boris Karloff (Baron von Leppe) Jack Nicholson (Andre Duvalier) Sandra Knight (Helene) Richard Miller (Stefan) Dorothy Neumann (Old Woman) Jonathan Haze (Gustaff)

THUNDER ISLAND
Associated Producers USA
Director: Jack Leewood **Producer:** Jack Leewood **Screenplay:** Jack Nicholson, Don Devlin **Photography:** John Nickolaus **Editor:** Jodie Copelan **Music:** Paul Sawtell, Bert Shefter **Cast:** Gene Nelson (Billy Poole) Fay Spain (Helen Dodge) Brian Kelly (Vincent Dodge) Miriam Colon (Anita Chavez) Art Bedard (Ramon Alou)

1964

ENSIGN PULVER
Warner Bros. USA
Director: Joshua Logan **Producer:** Joshua Logan **Screenplay:** Joshua Logan, Peter Feibleman (Using characters from the play Mr ROBERTS by Joshua Logan and Thomas Heggen) **Photography:** Charles Lawton **Editor:** William Reynolds **Music:** George Dunning **Cast:** Robert Walker Jr. (Pulver) Burl Ives (Captain) Walter Matthau (Doc) Millie Perkins (Scotty) Tommy Sands (Bruno) Kay Medford (Head Nurse) Jack Nicholson (Crew Member)

BACK DOOR TO HELL
Lippert / Medallion USA
Director: Monte Hellman **Producer:** Fred Roos **Screenplay:** Richard Guttman, John Hackett **Photography:** Mars Rasca **Editor:** Fely Crisotomo **Music:** Mike Velarde **Cast:** Jimmie Rodgers (Lt. Craig) Jack Nicholson (Burnett) John Hackett (Jersey) Annabelle Huggins (Maria) Conrad Maga (Paco) Johhny Monteiro (Ramundo) Joe Sison (Japanese Captain)

1966

FLIGHT TO FURY
Lippert / Inc.-Filipinas USA
Director: Monte Hellman **Producer:** Fred Roos **Screenplay:** Jack Nicholson (Based on a story by Monte Hellman, Fred Roos) **Photography:** Mike Accion **Cast:** Dewey Martin (Joe Gaines) Fay Spain (Destiny Cooper) Jack Nicholson (Jay Wickam)

Jacqueline Hellman (Gloria Walsh) Vic Diaz (Lorgren) Joseph Estrada (Garuda) John Hackett (Al Ross) Juliet Prado (Lei Ling)

THE SHOOTING
Santa Clara USA
Director: Monte Hellman **Producer:** Monte Hellman, Jack Nicholson **Screenplay:** Adrien Joyce **Photography:** Gregory Sandor **Editor:** Monte Hellman **Music:** Richard Markovitz **Cast:** Warren Oates (Willet Gashade) Will Hutchins (Coley) Millie Perkins (Woman) Jack Nicholson (Billy Spear) B.J. Merholz (Leland Drum) Cuy el Tsosie (Indian)

RIDE IN THE WHIRLWIND
Proteus USA
Director: Monte Hellman **Producer:** Monte Hellman, Jack Nicholson **Screenplay:** Jack Nicholson **Photography:** Gregory Sandor **Editor:** Monte Hellman **Music:** Robert Drasnin **Cast:** Cameron Mitchell (Vern) Jack Nicholson (Wes) Millie Perkins (Abby) Tom Fuler (Otis) Katherine Squire (Catherine) George Mitchell (Evan) Brandon Caroll (Sheriff)

1967

HELLS ANGELS ON WHEELS
Fanfare Films USA
Director: Richard Rush **Producer:** Joe Solomon **Screenplay:** R. Wright Campbell **Photography:** Lazlo Kovacs **Editor:** William Martin **Music:** Stu Phillips **Song:** 'Study In Motion No.1' Written by Chuck Sedacca, Stu Phillips, Performed by The Poor **Cast:** Jack Nicholson (Poet) Adam Rourke (Buddy) Sabrina Scharf (Shill) Jana Taylor (Abigale) John Garwood (Jock) Richard Anders (Bull) Mimi Machu (Pearl)

REBEL ROUSERS
Paragon International USA
Director: Martin B. Cohen **Producer:** Martin B. Cohen **Screenplay:** Abe Polsky, Michael Kars, Martin B. Cohen **Photography:** Lazlo Kovacs **Editor:** Thor Brooks **Music:** Cameron Mitchell (Mr Collier) Jack Nicholson ('Bunny') Bruce Dern ('J.J.') Diane Ladd (Karen) Dean Stanton, Neil Burstyn, Lou Procopio, Earl Finn, Philip Carey (The Rebels)

THE ST VALENTINE'S DAY MASSACRE
Los Altos USA
Director: Roger Corman **Producer:** Roger Corman **Screenplay:** Howard Browne **Photography:** Milton Krasner **Editor:** William B. Murphy **Music:** Lionel Newman, Fred Steiner **Cast:** Jason Robards Jr. (Al Capone) George Segal (Peter Gusenberg) Ralph Meeker (Bugs Moran) Jean Hale (Myrtle) Clint Ritchie (Jack McGurn) Frank Silvera (Sorello) Jack Nicholson (Driver of Getaway Car)

THE TRIP
A.I.P. USA
Director: Roger Corman **Producer:** Roger Corman **Screenplay:** Jack Nicholson **Photography:** Arch Dalzell **Editor:**

Ronald Sinclair **Music:** The Electric Flag **Cast:** Peter Fonda (Paul Groves) Susan Strasberg (Sally) Bruce Dern (John) Dennis Hopper (Max) Salli Sachse (Glenn) Katherine Walsh (Lulu) Barboura Morris (Flo)

1968

PSYCH-OUT
Dick Clark Productions USA
Director: Richard Rush **Producer:** Dick Clark **Screenplay:** E. Hunter Willett, Betty Ulius, (Based on a story by E. Hunter Willett) **Photography:** Lazlo Kovacs **Editor:** Ken Reynolds **Music:** Ronald Stein **Songs:** 'Psych-Out', 'Psych-Out Sanctorum', 'The Love Children' by Ronald Stein 'Beads Of Innocence' by Ronald and Harlene Stein 'The Pretty Song' by The Strawberry Alarm Clock performed by The Storybook. 'Innocence And Peppermints' by John Carter, Tim Gilbert 'Rainy Day Mushroom Pillow' by Steven Bartek, George Bunnell 'The World's On Fire' by The Strawberry Alarm Clock performed by The Strawberry Alarm Clock. 'Two Fingers Pointing On You' by Sky Saxon performed by The Seeds. 'Ashbury Wednesday' by R. Young, M. Mitchell, J. Neddo, G. Grantham, S. Bush performed by Boenze Cryque **Cast:** Susan Strasberg (Jennie) Dean Stockwell (Dave) Jack Nicholson (Stoney) Bruce Dern (Steve) Adam Rourke (Ben) Max Julien (Elwood) Henry Jaglom (Warren)

HEAD
Raybert Productions USA
Director: Bob Rafelson **Producer:** Bob Rafelson, Jack Nicholson **Screenplay:** Bob Rafelson, Jack Nicholson **Photography:** Michael Hugo **Editor:** Mike Pozen **Musical Director:** Ken Thorne **Music Co-ordinator:** Igo Cantor **Songs:** 'Porpoise Song' by Gerry Goffin, Carole King 'Circle Song' by Michael Nesmith 'Can You Dig It' by Peter Tork 'As We Go Along' by Carole King, Toni Stern 'Daddy's Song' by Nillsson 'Long Title: Do I Have To Do This All Over Again?' by Peter Tork **Cast:** Davy Jones, Mike Nesmith, Peter Tork, Micky Dolenz (The Monkees) Victor Mature ('The Big Victor') Annette Funicello (Minnie) Jack Nicholson, Bob Rafelson (as themselves)

1969

EASY RIDER
Pando Co./Raybert Productions USA
Director: Dennis Hopper **Producer:** Peter Fonda **Screenplay:** Peter Fonda, Dennis Hopper, Terry Southern **Photography:** Lazlo Kouacs **Editor:** Dawn Cambren **Music:** 'The Pusher', 'Born To Be Wild', 'I Wasn't Born To Follow', 'The Weight', 'If You Want To Be A Bird', 'Don't Bogart Me', 'If Six Was Nine', 'Let's Turkey Trot', 'Kyrie Eleison', 'Flash Bam Pow', 'Its Alright Ma (I'm Only Bleeding)', 'The Ballad Of Easy Rider'. Written by (variously): Gerry Goffin, Carole King, Jaime Robbie Robertson, Antonia Duren, Elliot Ingber, Larry Wagner, Jimi Hendrix, Jack Keller, David Axelrod, Mike Bloomfield, Bob Dylan and Roger McGuin. Performed by Steppenwolf, The

Byrds, The Band, The Holy Mondal Rounders, Fraternity of Man, The Jimi Hendrix Experience, Little Eva, The Electric Prunes, Electric Flag and Roger McGuin. **Cast:** Peter Fonda (Wyatt) Dennis Hopper (Billy) Jack Nicholson (George Hanson) Antonio Mendoza (Jesus) Phil Spector (Connection) Mac Mashourian (Body Guard)

1970

ON A CLEAR DAY YOU CAN SEE FOREVER
Paramount USA
Director: Vincente Minnelli **Producer:** Howard Koch **Screenplay:** Alan Jay Lerner (Based on his and Burton Lane's musical play) **Photography:** Harry Stradling **Editor:** David Bretherton **Musical Direction:** Nelson Riddle **Songs:** 'Hurry! It's Love Up There', 'On A Clear Day...', 'Melinda', 'He Wasn't You', 'What Did I Have, That I Don't Have Now?', 'Come Back To Me', 'Love With All The Trimmings', 'Go To Sleep'. Written by Burton Lane and Alan Jay Lerner. **Cast:** Barbra Streisand (Daisy Gamble) Yves Montand (Dr Marc Chabot) Bob Newhart (Dr Mason Hume) Larry Blyden (Warren Pratt) Jack Nicholson (Tad Pringle) Simon Oakland (Dr Conrad Fuller)

FIVE EASY PIECES
B.B.S. USA
Director: Bob Rafelson **Producer:** Bob Rafelson, Richard Wechsler **Screenplay:** Adrien Joyce (Based on a story by Adrien Joyce and Bob Rafelson) **Photography:** Lazlo Kovacs **Editor:** Christopher Holmes, Gerald Shepherd **Music:** Fantasy in F Minor Op.49/Prelude in E Minor Op.28 by Chopin. Piano Concerto in E Flat Major/Fantasy in D Minor by Mozart. Chromatic Fantasy and Fugue by Bach. Pearl Kaufman - Solo Piano **Songs:** 'Stand By Your Man' by B. Sherill, T. Wynette 'D-I-V-O-R-C-E' by B. Braddock, C. Putnam 'When There's A Fire In Your Heart' by W. Kilgore, S. Williams 'Don't Touch Me' by H. Cochran. Sung by Tammy Wynette **Cast:** Jack Nicholson (Robert Eroica Dupea) Karen Black (Rayette Dipesto) Lois Smith (Partita Dupea) Susan Anspach (Catherine Van Ost) Billy 'Green' Bush (Elton) Fannie Flagg (Stoney) Ralph Waite (Carl Fidelio Dupea)

DRIVE, HE SAID
B.B.S./Drive Productions USA
Director: Jack Nicholson **Producer:** Jack Nicholson, Steve Blauner **Screenplay:** Jack Nicholson, Jeremy Larner (Based on the novel by Jeremy Larner) **Photography:** Bill Butler **Editor:** Pat Somerset, Don Cambern, Chris Holmes, Robert Wolfe **Music:** David Shire — Title Theme: Louis Hardin **Songs:** 'I Cried For You' by Abe Lyman, Gus Arnheim, Arthur Freed. Sung by Billie Holliday 'Spaced' Written and performed by Beaver and Krause 'Classical Gas' Written and performed by Mason Williams **Cast:** William Tepper (Hector Bloom) Karen Black (Olive) Michael Margotta (Gabriel) Bruce Dern (Coach Bullion) Robert Towne (Richard Calvin) Henry Jaglom (Prof. Conrad) June Fairchild (Sylvie Mertens)

1971

CARNAL KNOWLEDGE
Icarus USA
Director: Mike Nichols **Producer:** Mike Nichols **Screenplay:** Jules Feiffer **Photography:** Guiseppe Rotunno **Editor:** Sam O'Steen **Music:** 'Moonlight Serenade' by Mitchell Paris, Glenn Miller 'I'm Getting Sentimental Over You' by N. Washington, G. Bassman 'Falling Leaves' by Mack David, Frankie Carle 'Tuxedo Junction' by E. Hawkins, W. Johnson, J. Dash, B. Feyne 'A String Of Pearls' by J. Gray, E. de Large 'Georgia On My Mind' by Hoagy Carmichael, Stuart Garrell 'Sari Waltz' by Emmerich Kalman 'I'm Coming Back To You' by Arthur Kent, Ed Warren. 'Der Rosen Kavalier Waltz' by Richard Strauss 'Dream' by Johnny Mercer 'I Walk Alone' by Jule Styne, Sammy Cahn 'I'll String Along With You' by Al Dubin, H. Warren 'La Paloma' by Yradier 'Ampala' by Joseph La Calle, Albert Gaurse 'Roga. Kedera. Alap Gat Taal Teental' by Kaiyan, Ali Ahmed Hussan 'St Matthew Passion' by Bach **Cast:** Jack Nicholson (Jonathan) Candice Bergen (Susan) Art Garfunkel (Sandy) Ann-Margret (Bobbie) Rita Moreno (Louise) Cynthia O'Neal (Cindy) Carol Kane (Jennifer)

A SAFE PLACE
B.B.S. for Columbia USA
Director: Henry Jaglom **Producer:** Bert Schneider **Screenplay:** Henry Jaglom **Photography:** Dick Kratina **Editor:** Peter Bergema **Music Consultant:** Jim Gitter **Songs:** 'As Time Goes By' by Herman Huffeld. Sung by Dooley Wilson 'La Vie En Rose' by R.S.Louiguy Sung by Edith Piaf 'Passing By' by Edward Purcell Sung by Buddy Clarke 'Someone To Watch Over Me' by George and Ira Gershwin Sung by Dinah Shore 'Lavender Blue' by Eliot Daniel and Larry Morey Sung by Vera Lynn 'Vous Qui Passez Sans Me Voir' and 'La Mer' Written and performed by Charles Trenet 'Something to Remember You By' by Arthur Schwartz, Howard Dietz Sung by Helen Forrest 'I'm Old Fashioned' by Jerome Kern and Johnny Mercer Sung by Fred Astaire 'Its A Big Wide Wonderful World' by John Rox Sung by Buddy Clark **Cast:** Tuesday Weld (Susan) Jack Nicholson (Mitch) Orson Welles (Magician) Philip Proctor (Fred) Gwen Welles (Bari) Dov Lawrence (Larry)

1972

THE KING OF MARVIN GARDENS
B.B.S. USA
Director: Bob Rafelson **Producer:** Bob Rafelson **Screenplay:** Jacob Brackman (Based on a story by Jacob Brackman and Bob Rafelson) **Photography:** Lazlo Kovacs **Editor:** John. F. Link II **Music Supervision:** Synchrofilm Inc. **Cast:** Jack Nicholson (David Staebler) Bruce Dern (Jason Staebler) Ellen Burstyn (Sally) Julia Anne Robinson (Jessica) 'Scatman' Crothers (Lewis) Charles Levine (Grandfather)

1974

THE LAST DETAIL
Acrobat/Bright-Persky Assoc. USA
Director: Hal Ashby **Producer:** Gerald Ayres **Screenplay:** Robert Towne (Based on the novel by Darryl Ponicsan) **Photography:** Michael Chapman **Editor:** Robert Jones **Music:** Johnny Mandel **Songs:** 'Never Let The Left Hand Know', 'Sing Us Another Song' by Jack Goga 'Good Ole Country Living', 'Nothin' Ever Stays the Same' by Jack Goga, K Lawrence Dunham 'Don't Believe It', 'Please Come Back' By Ron Nagel 'Bad Ass Blues' by Miles Goodman 'Something You Still Haven't Said' by Miles Goodman, Douglas Brayfield **Cast:** Jack Nicholson (Billy 'Bad Ass' Buddusky) Otis Young ('Mule' Mulhall) Randy Quaid (Larry Meadows) Clifton James (M.A.A.) Carol Kane (Young Whore) Michael Moriarty (Marine O.D.) Luana Anders (Donna)

CHINATOWN
Long Road Productions USA
Director: Roman Polanski **Producer:** Robert Evans **Screenplay:** Robert Towne **Photography:** John A. Alonzo **Editor:** Sam O'Steen **Music:** Jerry Goldsmith **Songs:** 'I Can't Get Started' by Vernon Duke, Ira Gershwin 'Love Is Just Around The Corner' by Leo Robin, Lewis Gensler 'Easy Living' by Leo Robin, Ralph Rainger 'The Way You Look Tonight' by Jerome Kern, Dorothy Fields 'Some Day The Vagabound King Waltz' by Rudolf Friml, Brian Hooker **Cast:** Jack Nicholson (J.J. Gittes) Faye Dunaway (Evelyn Mulwray) John Huston (Noah Cross) Perry Lopez (Escobar) Dianne Ladd (Ida Sessions) Darrell Zwerling (Hollis Mulwray) John Hillerman (Yelburton)

1975

PROFESSIONE: REPORTER (THE PASSENGER)

CCC (Rome)/LFC(Paris)/Cipic (Madrid) Italy/France/Spain
Director: Michelangelo Antonioni **Producer:** Carlo Ponti **Screenplay:** Mark Peploe, Peter Wollen, Michelangelo Antonioni **Photography:** Luciano Tovoli **Editor:** Franco Arcalli, Michelangelo Antonioni **Music Advisor:** Ivan Vardor **Cast:** Jack Nicholson (David Locke) Maria Schneider (Girl) Jenny Runacre (Rachel Locke) Ian Hendry (Martin Knight) Stephen Berkoff (Stephen) James Campbell (Witch Doctor) Ambrose Bia (Achebe)

TOMMY
Robert Stigwood Organization GB
Director: Ken Russell **Producer:** Ken Russell, Robert Stigwood **Screenplay:** Ken Russell (Based on the rock opera 'Tommy') **Photography:** Dick Bush, Ronnie Taylor **Editor:** Stuart Bird **Musical Direction:** Pete Townshend **Songs:** 'Capt. Walker Didn't Come Home', 'Its A Boy!', 'The Acid Queen', '51 Is Going To Be A Good Year', 'What About The Boy?', 'See Me, Feel Me', 'The Amazing Journey', 'Christmas', 'Do You Think It's Alright?', 'Cousin Kevin', 'Fiddle About', 'Sparks', 'Pinball Wizard', 'Today It Rained Champagne', 'There's A Doctor', 'Go To The Mirror', 'Tommy Can You Hear Me', 'Smash The Mirror', 'I'm Free', 'Miracle Cure', 'Sensation', 'Sally Simpson', 'Welcome', 'Tommy's Holiday Camp', 'Deceived', 'We're Not Gonna Take It', 'Listening To You' Written by Pete Townshend and The Who 'Eyesight To The Blind' Written by Sonny Boy Williamson **Musicians:** Elton John, Eric Clapton, Keith Moon, John Entwhistle, Ronnie Wood, Kenny Jones, Nicky Hopkins, Chris Stanton, Fuzzy Samuels, Caleb Quayle, Mick Ralphs, Graham Deakin, Phil Chan, Alan Ross, Richard Bailey, Dave Clinton, Tony Newman, Mike Kelly. Dee Murray, Nigel Olson, Ray Cooper, Geoff Daley, Davey Johnstone, Bob Effard, Ronnie Ross, Howie Casey, Gerald Shaw **Cast:** Ann-Margret (Nora Walker) Oliver Reed (Frank Hobbs) Roger Daltry (Tommy) Elton John (Pinball Wizard) Eric Clapton (Preacher) Keith Moon (Uncle Ernie) Jack Nicholson (Doctor)

THE FORTUNE
Columbia USA
Director: Mike Nichols **Producer:** Hank Moonjean **Screenplay:** Adrien Joyce (Carel Eastman) **Photography:** John A. Alonzo **Editor:** Stu Linder **Music:** David Shire **Songs:** 'I Must Be Dreaming' by A Dubin, P Flaherty, Al Sherman 'Petty Trix' by Joe Venuti, Eddie Lang 'My Honey's Lovin' Arms' by J Meyer, Herman Ruby **Cast:** Jack Nicholson (Oscar) Warren Beatty (Nicky) Stockard Channing (Freddie) Florence Stanley (Mrs Gould) Richard Shull (Chief Detective) Tom Newman (John The Barber)

ONE FLEW OVER THE CUCKOO'S NEST
Fantasy Films USA
Director: Milos Forman **Producer:** Saul Zaentz, Michael Douglas **Screenplay:** Lawrence Hauben, Bo Goldman (Based on the novel by Ken Kesey)

Photography: Bill Butler, William Fraker
Editor: Lynzee Klingman, Sheldon Kahn
Music: Jack Nitzche **Cast:** Jack
Nicholson (R.P. McMurphy) Louise
Fletcher (Nurse Ratched) William Redfield
(Harding) Will Sampson (Chief Bromden)
Brad Dourif (Billy Bibbit) Marya Small
(Candy) Sydney Lassick (Cheswick)
'Scatman' Crothers (Turkle)

1976

THE MISSOURI BREAKS
E.K. Exec USA
Director: Arthur Penn **Producer:** Robert
Sherman **Screenplay:** Thomas McGuane
Photography: Michael Butler **Editor:**
Jerry Greenberg, Stephen Rotter, Dede
Allen **Music:** John Williams **Cast:** Marlon
Brando (Robert Lee Clayton) Jack
Nicholson (Tom Logan) Randy Quaid
(Little Tod) Kathleen Lloyd (Jane Braxton)
Frederick Forrest (Cary) Harry Dean
Stanton (Calvin) John McLiam (David
Braxton)

THE LAST TYCOON
Academy for Paramount USA
Director: Elia Kazan **Producer:** Sam
Spiegel **Screenplay:** Harold Pinter (Based
on the novel by F. Scott Fitzgerald)
Photography: Victor Kemper **Editor:**
Richard Marks **Music:** Maurice Jarre
Cast: Robert De Niro (Monroe Starr)
Ingrid Boulting (Kathleen Moore) Robert
Mitchum (Pat Brady) Jeanne Moreau
(Didi) Jack Nicholson (Brimmer) Tony
Curtis (Rodriguez) Donald Pleasence
(Boxley) Ray Milland (Fleischacher) Dana
Andrews (Red Riding Hood) Teresa
Russell (Cecilia Brady)

1979

GOIN' SOUTH
Paramount USA
Director: Jack Nicholson **Producer:**
Harry Gittes, Harold Schneider
Screenplay: John Herman Sharer, Al
Ramus, Charles Shyer, Alan Mandel
Photography: Nestor Almendros **Editor:**
Richard Chew, John Fitzgerald Beck
Music: Van Dyke Parks, Perry Botkin Jnr.
Songs: 'Available Space' written and
performed by Ry Cooder 'Scarf Dance' by
Cecile Chaminade performed by Bob and
Enoch Westmoreland **Cast:** Jack
Nicholson: (Henry Lloyd Moon) Mary
Steenburgen (Julia Tate) Christopher
Lloyd (Frank Towfield) John Belushi
(Hector) Veronica Cartwright (Hermine)
Richard Bradford (Sheriff Andrew Kyle)
Jeff Morris (Big Abe)

THE SHINING
Hawk Films GB
Director: Stanley Kubrick **Producer:**
Stanley Kubrick **Screenplay:** Stanley
Kubrick, Diane Johnson (Based on the
novel by Stephen King) **Photography:**
John Alcott **Editor:** Ray Lovejoy **Music:**
Music for Strings, Percussion and Celesta
by Bela Bartok, Conducted by Herbert
von Karajan. Ad. Music: Wendy Carlos,
Rachel Elking, Gyorgy Ligeti, Krzysztof
Penderecki **Cast:** Jack Nicholson (Jack
Torrance) Shelley Duvall (Wendy
Torrance) Danny Lloyd (Danny Torrance)
'Scatman' Crothers (Dick Halloran) Barry
Nelson (Stuart Ullmann) Philip Stone
(Delbert Grady) Joe Turkel (Lloyd)

1981
THE POSTMAN ALWAYS RINGS TWICE
Lorimar USA
Director: Bob Rafelson **Producer:** Bob
Rafelson, Charles Mulvehill **Screenplay:**
David Mamet (Based on the novel by
James. M. Cain) **Photography:** Sven
Nykvist **Editor:** Graeme Clifford **Music:**
Director: Michael Small Orchestration:
Jack Hayes Editor: Dan Carlin **Cast:** Jack
Nicholson (Frank Chambers) Jessica
Lange (Cora Papadakis) John Colicos
(Nick Papadakis) Michael Lerner (Katz)
John Ryan (Kennedy) Angelica Huston
(Madge) Jon Van Ness (Motorcycle Cop)

REDS
Paramount USA
Director: Warren Beatty **Producer:**
Warren Beatty **Screenplay:** Warren
Beatty, Trevor Griffiths **Photography:**
Vittorio Storaro **Editor:** Dede Allen, Craig
McKay **Music:** Stephen Sondheim
Additional Music: Dave Grusin **Songs:**
'You're A Grand Old Flag', 'Over There',
Yankee Doodle Boy' by George M. Cohan
'Cartoon Rag' by Michael Karp 'Onward
Christian Soldiers' by S. Baring-Gould, A.
Sullivan 'Waiting For The Robert E. Lee'
by L. Wolfe Gilbert, Louis F. Muir
'Liebesfreud' by Fritz Kreisler 'I Don't
Want To Play In Your Yard' by P.
Wingate, H.W. Petrie 'Oh, You Beautiful
Doll' by A.S.Brown, Nat Ayer 'America
The Beautiful' by Katherine Bates, Samuel
Ward 'St Louis Tickle' by B., S. & G
Snelgrove 'Dill Pickles' by Charles L.
Johnson 'Rattlesnake Rag' by Louis Bush,
Eddy Hanson 'Stop Your Ticklin' Me' by
Jack Little, Walter Hirsch 'The Crazy Otto
Rag' by E. White, M. Wolfson, L.
Creatore, H. Peretti 'Just A Little Love
Song' by J. Young, Sam Lewis, Joe
Cooper 'The Internationale' by Pierre
Degeyter, Eugene Pottier 'Country Club-
Ragtime Two-Step' by Scott Joplin.
Performed by J. Rifkin 'The Engine' and
'The Red Army Is The Most Powerful Of
All' Performed by The Moscow Radio
Chorus **Cast:** Warren Beatty (John Reed)
Diane Keaton (Louise Bryant) Edward
Herrmann (Max Eastman) Jerzy Kosinski
(Grigory Zonoviev) Jack Nicholson
(Eugene O'Neill) Paul Sorvino (Louis
Fraina) Maureen Stapleton (Emma
Goldman) Nicolas Coster (Paul Trullinger)
Ian Wolfe (Mr Partlow) Bessie Love (Mrs
Partlow) Gene Hackman (Pete Van
Wherry) **Witnesses:** Roger Baldwin
Henry Miller Arthur Mayer Adela Rogers
St. John Dora Russell Scott Nearing Tess
Davis Heaton Vorse Hamilton Fish Isaac
Don Levine Rebecca West Will Durant
Will Weinstone Oleg Kerensky Emmanuel
Herbert Arne Swabeck Adele Nathan
George Seldes Kenneth Chamberlain
George Jessel Harry Carlisle Art Shields
Galina von Meck Andrew Dasburg Hugo
Gellert Jacob Bailin John Ballato Lucita
Williams

THE BORDER
Universal USA
Director: Tony Richardson **Producer:**
Edgar Bronfman **Screenplay:** Deric
Washburn, Walon Green (Based on a
story by Deric Washburn) **Photography:**
Ric Waite **Editor:** Robert K. Lambert
Cast: Jack Nicholson (Charlie) Valerie
Perrine (Marcy) Harvey Keitel (Cat)
Warren Oates (Big Red) Elpidia Carrillo
(Maria) Shannon Wilcox (Savannah)